Learn Agile and Scrum software development in an enjoyable and memorable way

The following concepts are covered in this dramatic story: Agile Manifesto values and principals, the Scrum framework, history of Waterfall, user stories, Planning Poker estimation, cross–team dependencies, Scrum of Scrums, and the challenges of organizational change.

Kartar Patel

. . . a savvy project manager who is determined, disciplined, and and above all, handsome. He's got a high profile project for a Vegas casino and puts his heart and soul into delivering the Winner. But when timelines are slipped, stakeholders want a pound of flesh for every ounce of letdown. He's being followed . . . discovers tracking devices on his car . . . his meetings are bugged . . . he gets a gun. A mysterious stranger tells him he'll never succeed without transforming his project to an Agile process. Kartar discovers that not only his career and life are on the line, but so is his immortal soul.

Lance(r) Kind

. . . an Agile consultant and science fiction author who consults in the USA, China, and India at many famous Fortune 100 companies. His works include: SCRUM NOIR, MEMORY'S VICTIMS, CAVEMAN FUNK, BIT STORM, and HONOLULU HOTTIE. The last two awarded Honorable Mention by Writers of the Future. The first is a project management comic book series about Scrum.

Comics and Novelettes by Lancer Kind

Memory's Victims
Honolulu Hottie
Caveman Funk
Bit Storm
SCRUM NOIR: A Silo To Hell! episodes 1–3
SCRUM NOIR: Mad Dog Mary episodes 1–3
SCRUM NOIR: Bad Boys of Scrum episodes 1–3

All the above are available at various online and in-store
book sellers.

Agile Noir

LANCER KIND

This is a work of fiction. Names, characters, places, and incidents are either the product of the author's imagination or are used fictitiously, and any resemblance to actual persons, living or dead, business establishments, events, or locales is entirely coincidental. If you see similarities between yourself and the hero, congratulations! If you identify most strongly to a villain, find a hero and work things out.

US: 13

ISBN–10: 1533516499

ISBN–13: 978–1533516497

DEDICATION

To those who make change possible despite organizational antibodies. Support the good struggle, listen to those building the asset, and find ways to make change <u>their</u> idea.

CONTENTS

ACKNOWLEDGMENTS

As a good host, let me first introduce contributors, Ebin John Poovathany, and then Deepak Dhananjaya and Gunjan Zutshi. Ebin shares a slice of the coach's life with: Agile Development is about having Fun! Deepak and Gunjan share their organizational transformation strategy in: Why Let Your Framework Limit You?

The cover art was done by Fauji M. Bardah, a talented artist from Indonesia whom I've had the pleasure of working with for the covers of many of my science fiction novelettes. The interior illustrations were hand drawn by my lovely wife Lilian.

Many thanks to dear friend and colleague Nagaraja Ramaiah, also known as 'King Cobra,' for showing me around Bangaluru, India and answering my incessant questions on Hindu mythology. For questions he couldn't answer, he arranged a visit to an Indian guru at the Ramakrishna Math who patiently listened to my story outline.

To all the great people who I have rubbed elbows with when coaching teams, thank you for making me smarter.
And finally, to those who never agreed with anything I said, thank you for making me tougher and, most of all, inspiring dramatic villainy.

THE HIGH COST OF SCHEDULE SLIP

'Adventure is the result of bad planning,' Kartar texted to his daughter. It was a quote he'd stolen from someone famous. In one hand was his phone, in his jacket pocket was breakfast of a napkin wrapped thepla, and in his other hand was a go-cup of steaming hot chai. Although busy with his phone, he didn't spill a drop rushing down the stairs or tripping on a pizza box left on the floor. He even managed to get the door to the garage open without setting anything down. 'Please toss pizza box! Txt me today's plan. In garage now.'

She responded, 'Awe! I hear the garage opening. I was just lying in bed! You could've said good morning.'

'Sorry. If you want to go out, there's a bus to downtown every hour. But tell me before you go.'

Kartar got into his Acura and set his BlackBerry to full text–to–voice. As he backed out of the garage, the chrome phone vibrated and chimed, signaling he'd received another text message. A robotic voice came over the car's speakers.

"From Dharma. Stop being such a planner boy. I'll be

11

home watching movies and playing video games. See? A plan. I'll sit home, bored, waiting for you. Hope you don't come home so late again. I don't want pizza for dinner all summer."

The neighborhood was new, sitting on the edge of Las Vegas with desert views all around. He steered with his knee while sipping chai and eating the thepla, its crust soggy from being microwaved. Although the BlackBerry buzzed the arrival of the morning's emails, he adjusted the phone to hear what had arrived at 11 pm the night before.

Sounding like a robot from an old science fiction movie, the BlackBerry read messages from the test team in India. The Winner was running very late, now scheduled to release a year from today. This month it's been stalled in Test. Last night, the same bad news: testers blocked because their environment wouldn't work.

Email after email, filled with questions about what the system should look like when working, what processes should be running, how long the hardware emulator should take to start. Cries for help during a storm, cries which no one was awake to hear until eight hours later, when the Vegas teams started work.

". . . Despite all efforts, the user interface comes up as a blank window, no matter what we do. Per the server team's documentation, we opened tickets with our operators to have the server rebooted. When the server came up, we filed a ticket with the operators to check that the correct services were running, and they were. Everything looks correct to the operators, per the documentation we got from the architecture and server teams."

Kartar stopped at a three–way intersection. The interstate and the path to work on the left; to the right, an unfinished extension of the neighborhood, street and sidewalk extending into empty desert. Nothing moved in the late morning heat except, a block back, a van pulled over. It had been in the neighborhood lately. One of those promotional wraps around its body, advertising the Topless Revue at Caesar's.

The emails from the Test team continued.

"So we then move to the UI team's documentation."

Kartar stayed at the stop sign, set fingers on the chest of his polo shirt, shaping fabric around a ring that hung from a chain beneath. He pinched the ring, holding his breath and hoping last night's test holdup wasn't his team's fault.

"At first, even launching the hardware emulator failed, but last night, we got an email from a member of the Wow team that a configuration filename had changed. We corrected that problem. Also, the email told us about an undocumented command line argument. After that, the emulator came up."

He slapped his forehead and wondered how many times he'd asked his developers if the documentation was up to date. They always answered, "Yes." "Bad Wow," he said to himself.

"But when the user interface starts, we only get a blank screen. We still don't have a working system to test but are further along."

Further along, Kartar thought, but by now we'd hoped to finish a pass of tests and turned around fixes.

A car horn blared and Kartar jumped. The van's grill filled the rear–view.

"OK, OK, hold your shorts."

As he set his foot on the gas, the van moved abreast. Kartar pressed the brake, unsure what the driver intended. The Nude Review ad on the van was a woman in a top hat, her white gloved hands covering the ends of her breasts. She seemed to stare at him.

"I'm sure the show is tasteful." He shook his head.

The van was still, as if it waited for him. He started into the intersection. The van did the same, flanking him, blocking his turn toward the interstate. He glanced at the van, his car only inches from the woman in white gloves and top hat. The van swerved at him. He veered away and the BlackBerry slid across the dash to bang into the windshield. The robot voice was undeterred and read on about how all testing was blocked because the system wouldn't work.

He continued in the wrong direction, the van alongside and on the wrong side of the road. Even with the accelerator to the floor, the van kept pace. Ahead, the road ended in an empty cul–de–sac and shimmering desert.

I should have leased the Caddy, he thought to himself. Too expensive to buy, but could've leased it. The Cadillac V8 would have blown this sucker away.

Roaring down the road, he shot a glance toward the van, trying to gauge what to do. The front seat window was tinted but he could see the shadow of a passenger. The van was larger and they outnumbered him. Probably High schoolers screwing around.

At seventy miles per hour, the dead end came fast. He stood on the brakes. Nearby, the van skidded to a stop. They were listening to music . . . something with violins.

Ahead, the curb was sloped low for a future driveway, but right now, only led to desert. Nobody nearby to help with these lunatics; only sand, faded plastic bags, and rocks. His neighborhood, visible through the rear–view, seemed far away.

Although impossible to see the license plate, he grabbed his Blackberry and readied his thumbs, waiting for the van to budge.

"You'll move eventually."

Waiting and more waiting, the show advertisement looming above. He fantasized that inside were topless performers for the Nude Revue then shook his head because he'd never be so lucky—it was probably a rolling meth lab. And they'd have guns. But classical music?

The van shifted ever so slightly and the music became clear: flutes and strings, orchestral Irish step, maybe Lord of the Dance. Someone must have opened their door and exited, and likely stood on the other side. He watched and wondered what their game was.

The BlackBerry vibrated that new email had arrived. The robot voice came over the speaker again.

"From DeLucca: We can't keep slipping the schedule on a project that's already a year late. Casino De'Arte has its future riding on the Winner being the first handheld gambling device. Be at my office at 11 and bring the latest Gantt."

He groaned. Why must people with titles like "President of Casino Gaming" always call meetings on such short notice? Thirty minutes to make the meeting, but a forty–minute commute. And that's if he were on the interstate now.

He almost missed seeing the shadow of someone sneaking at the back of the van. Something suspicious was up and he'd enough.

He tossed the phone onto the dash and popped the clutch. Tires squealed over blacktop, and over the curb and into the desert the car jounced, slipping and catching traction on rock–strewn sand. The tach hit the red–line. Kartar shifted into second and put the pedal down hard, driving as his life depended on it. He had to keep moving. Lose momentum, and he'd get stuck. Glanced at the rear–view; from the rear of the van the skulker, a woman, watched him.

Dirt flew from front wheels as he tore over gravel and

troughs left by annual rains. The jolts tossed him against the seat belt. The car bounced over something hard and slew sideways. His head slammed against the door window.

Steering was by approximation: don't turn too sharp and get stuck, and don't keep going straight—farther into the desert and further from help. Safety meant distance from the van, but escape lay back at the intersection. A large detour through the desert, steering in shallow arcs like a boat traveling through choppy water.

A ditch, invisible until too late, yawned ahead—both front wheels dropped in. The car slammed its front into the bank and the world rushed forward, eyes focused on the steering wheel, body flying forward, accelerator still held to the floor. The shoulder belt jerked him to a stop—nose inches from smashing into the wheel. The desert scraped and kicked the car bottom as it lurched over the bank and surged forward.

Enough of this, he decided, and reversed course for the nearest blacktop which unfortunately meant returning toward the van he'd been trying to leave. As he approached, its cargo door slid close covering a second woman with a hawkish nose and blonde hair. He maneuvered for rocky dirt, hoping to avoid sand pits. "Keep moving. Keep moving." Get away or become a newspaper's sad ending: His daughter, alone in Vegas, answering the door to police notifying her that daddy had been shot dead by two women high on meth.

The car ricocheted over the sidewalk and surged into the air above the street. He floated upward, seat belt tensioning across his body, ring slipping free from his V-neck, floating before his face until the car returned to the earth, himself dropping into the seat.

Tires squealed on the blacktop. He fought for control and accelerated away from the van. It diminished in rearview, and after the three–way intersection, was lost from sight.

#

Kartar entered the President's office as Noah and Donny taped the Gantt to the wall, sheets of paper stretching from the doorway to the other side of the room alongside pictures of various antique slots and a photo of Mr. DeLucca golfing with Sylvester Stallone. The chart had become huge. No single person could completely understand it.

"Sorry I'm late," Kartar said. "Traffic problems."

The damp paper towels held to his bruised temple failed to garner sympathy.

"Traffic?" Mr. DeLucca said. "This is Vegas baby. Traffic may work as an excuse in California, but in Vegas, we've only got traffic on the Strip. And that, my friend, turns into money rolling through our doors."

"What happened to your noggin?" Donny said.

"Some crazy kids in a van. I should've called the cops."

"Kartar," Mr. DeLucca said. "Noah volunteered to fly one of his team to help fix Test's environment."

Noah sat cross–legged on the floor in front of the door; he wore his usual black pants and black shirt. Today's shirt had 'Got Root?' written in white. Donny sat in a chair that seemed much too small for his six–foot–four linebacker frame. Revo sunglasses perched on his bald, well–tanned head, attired in his usual scheme: a collared shirt with floral print and enough pastels to scream 'FLORIDA.'

"We've got a big problem." Mr. DeLucca darted to the end of the chart, his unbuttoned suit jacket flaring back, showing the designer label on the side of his silk shirt. He stabbed his finger at the line on the Gantt where it showed the time remaining to finish the project. "We've got a big problem!

"This is unacceptable. Last month, the chart showed the release date as being exactly one year from then. And after a month of trying to get the Winner through Test, the line is now a year and TWO MONTHS late. How the hell do we spend one month working on something, and end up adding TWO MORE to the schedule?"

DeLucca slapped the chart. "Am I even reading this damn thing right?"

Noah stood up, sighed, and walked to the chart. He started with the 'patience' voice, which Noah reserved for management.

"So the Gantt[1] chart has two axes. The horizontal represents time, which is why it stretches half the length of the office. This first line is the project line, the cumulative effort we've spent and will be spending. And yes, it shows that we've spent one year on it and it'll be at least another year and two more months before the happy day."

Kartar wondered briefly why Noah hadn't simply said, 'yes,' that DeLucca's read was correct. He was up to something. Kartar jotted down a summary of the chart to prepare a defense.

Noah said, "Beneath the project line are three more horizontal lines, each representing the teams Wow, Ka–Ching, and Arch. The length of each represents how long the team spent working, and those three lines sum up to the project line. The arrows between the lines are integration events between two teams. At our computers, we can drill in further and get task level details."

---

1   The chart is commonly known after Henry Gantt (1861–1919), who designed his chart around the years 1910–1915 (Wikipedia)

Here it comes, Kartar thought. Noah's going to complain about the GUI architecture. Better head it off, he decided. "If you're going to talk about all the back and forth between Wow and Arch, I'd like to remind you that would've been greatly reduced if you had agreed to my GUI architecture design. Whenever Wow added a new on–screen component, we had to meet with Arch and wait for them to release—"

Noah spun around to face them. "But I don't believe it," he said looking at Kartar. "I don't believe this chart," he said looking at Donny and DeLucca.

DeLucca shook his head. "Alright Matlock, you don't believe what? The chart? The end date? What?"

"Look at today's date and note that the Arch team doesn't have work for the rest of the project. Ka–Ching's wrapped up last month. Only Kartar's team and the Test team have work remaining. They're the long pole in the tent."

Kartar braced for a fight. Noah was trying to lay blame at his feet. He shook his head. "The bulk of requirement changes were in the UI. That's why Wow is still wrapping things up."

Noah nodded, deep nods that caused his long hair to swish forward. "Yes, yes. And that on–going work will turn into requirements changes for the Arch team. So I suspect that, within the week, the Arch team will have more work to do. I suspect Ka–Ching will also need to respond to changes driven by team Wow. So during each week of continued development, we'll discover more work and the Gantt will continue to grow."

DeLucca's face changed from normal to an ugly gray as Noah returned to his seat on the floor.

"What the hell's going on here?" DeLucca said. He reached into an inside breast pocket and pulled out a small black comb, which told his audience he didn't really want an answer to his question. After all, how could that slicked–back, Italian hair ever be out of place? Mr. DeLucca talked while pacing.

"All those slots on the gaming floor, and every two years you gotta replace them all with something new, some flashier machine. Because while the Strip may have traffic, that traffic could just as easily head to the casino up the block, or the one across the street, or pass us by completely to visit that goddamn, gargantuan MGM Grand.

"A casino's games is what brings 'em in. The job's easy. You give them something flashy and new to play with, and they have a good time dropping some dollars. As long as we give 'em a reason to stop, everyone's happy."

Mr. DeLucca slid his comb across the chart. "This, gentlemen, isn't making anyone happy. Not our guests, not our owners, not our management, and certainly not me.

"We're two times over budget. Our one–year project has become a two–year project, and now you three jokers are telling me, the more time we spend working, the more work we'll find? Casino De'Arte can't afford this. The other casinos can add floor space to bring in more revenue. Look at the MGM Grand! When they built, there was nothing, NOTHING around them. But us, we're surrounded."

Mr. DeLucca slapped the Gantt chart. "We got to work smarter!" He glared at each.

"So how do we bring in more revenue? We make the games smaller. Games you can carry around in your goddamn hand and play while lying in bed, inside the lounge, sitting on the john. We get rid of all those clunker slots and put in couches and cocktail tables. We do that, and we'll pull in a revenue–per–square–foot that's unheard of!"

As usual during a DeLucca moment of passion, white foam began to form in the corner of his mouth.

"I've people ready to remodel the game floor: curtain suppliers, furniture manufacturers, interior decorators. Marketing wants to promote the hell out of this launch. There'll be girls, gentlemen, girls with long legs and nice figures. We're getting the goddamn Rockettes! All twelve troupes will be here to put on a revue on the gaming floor. This'll be bigger than opening night of New York New York, with their Cirque du Soleil and that pack of flying monkeys.

But all this planning—contracts for labor, purchase orders for new sofas, tables, carpeting—all of it slips with the Winner."

Mr. DeLucca slapped the chart again and the picture of Stallone fell. The frame crashed face down, shattering the glass. Noah scooted further from hanging pictures.

"Jesus people!" Mr. DeLucca leveled his comb at them. "You need to think about more than yourselves!"

Kartar straightened in his chair and so did Donny, who didn't look like a relaxed Floridian at all. Noah remained unperturbed, as if he'd seen it all before at his 'super–duper high–tech' Bay Area jobs.

Mr. DeLucca banged on the wall. "No!" he said, beating on the wall with each word. "No! No! No!" Pictures slipped askew.

DeLucca gestured as if to stop traffic. "You know what? Do think of yourselves people! Do! Because those same money guys who loan to the desperate of the Strip? Those who give money to guests down on their luck, the ones who go after people's legs if they aren't happy? Well that's not too far from the truth for us as well. Our financiers have given us a great deal of money for something we should've already finished, and they want to know when they're going to receive compensation for their capital. Now you're telling me the more we work, the later the launch? These people aren't exactly nice guys. They'll want some heads to roll and it's not gonna be mine!"

Kartar tried not to stare at the white froth now at both corners of DeLucca's mouth. Clearly the Winner was DeLucca's first software project, because a year late for something brand–new was typical.

Kartar glanced at his coworkers, looking for support in settling DeLucca down. But even Donny, a rock in any storm, held eyebrows so high that his Revos looked like they sat on a washboard. Even Noah, Mr. 'I'm so skilled, I can snap my fingers and get a better job,' watched DeLucca with one hand frozen in mid–pull of his pony tail.

For the first time, Kartar wondered that maybe this job wouldn't be the one that got him his dream of being on the cover of WIRED magazine. Maybe he'd just get fired, or something worse if DeLucca was serious. But this wasn't the 1980s. People in IT didn't get their legs broken for late projects. In the software biz, late deliveries were just the nature of the beast.

DeLucca wiped hand across mouth and put his comb away.

"Alright, now that I have your attention, I'm confident there's a way out. We just need to take it a day at a time, and no more slips. So what's the problem with Test?"

Kartar looked at Donny for an indication that now was the time to assure DeLucca this was the way these projects tended to go. To stop freaking and calm down because most software projects run late and over budget, so organizations simply plan to ship late. But Donny's face was as blank as a poker player at the high stakes table, and Noah's eyes darted between Kartar and Donny, waiting for their lead. Kartar went to the Gantt chart, pleased that Noah couldn't just 'tech' his way out of this one. It was going to take management savvy to handle DeLucca.

Mr. DeLucca licked his lips but a fleck of white stayed.

Kartar brushed his thumb down a sideburn, focusing on the bristle sound the hairs made, then said, "You know, most projects finish late. Microsoft Windows XP, Microsoft Windows Vista, were both—"

Donny said, "If Test's system won't work, then why can't we do testing here, on our system?"

Mouth hanging open, Kartar was annoyed and amazed by Donny's out–of–the–box suggestion. Maybe that's what it took to wear shirts like Donny's.

Mr. DeLucca nodded. "Yeah, great idea. Let's make a project that's already late and over budget, further over budget by hiring expensive U.S. labor."

Donny dropped his gaze while Mr. DeLucca paced, his suit, his slick black hair, the concentration, all like coach Pat Riley pacing in front of the L.A. Laker's bench when down ten points in the fourth quarter. The face of someone who'd win at any cost. Kartar took comfort in that they played for the same team because he too needed this win.

Mr. DeLucca flipped the comb over his knuckles again and again as he stood there, staring. Each time, the comb traveled from his pointer finger and weaved between each digit, ending at the pinky.

"Oh!" DeLucca snapped his fingers, catching the comb in his other hand. "Crate up our system and ship it to India!"

Donny stared at the floor, shaking his head. Noah squinted at Mr. DeLucca, wondering if he'd heard wrong.

Kartar's heart pounded at the disaster this would

cause.

"How are the development teams going to get anything done? They need that system."

"But we're Development complete. Your software development life cycle says we're inside the Test Phase. You don't need the environment anymore," Mr. DeLucca said.

Donny still stared at the floor. Noah sat frozen. Kartar tried to decide where to start. More than most projects, their use of the Waterfall SDLC was a loose guideline at best. The directors driving the requirements would never declare the Requirements Phase 'complete.' Changes were slipped in here and there, causing even larger changes downstream: Specification, Design, Development, Test, and Implementation. More meetings, more documentation to update, more documentation to approve. One step forward, two steps back.

Donny looked up. "Shipping the environment is a good idea Mr. DeLucca, but if we ship it and Test sends us a bug report, how are we going to build a fix without a development environment?"

Noah nodded. "It would take weeks to get a replacement requisitioned, shipped, and the software installed."

"You're telling me that although I want the Gantt chart to be no longer than the Strip, it's going to be longer than I15?"

Noah stretched his arms while he said, "We could share our environment over the internet."

Kartar said, "We can't. The testers need their workstations attached to the server via USB, as required by the hardware emulator."

"Hardware emulator?" Mr. DeLucca said.

"Because the vendor was still developing the hardware, we used a computer program that operates as if it's the hardware so we can start testing. Our first hardware arrives in a few days."

Noah finished his stretch. Placing palms together, he rested his chin on fingertips, like some sort of guru. "This wouldn't be a problem if Wow had used a thick client with off–the–shelf hardware as I had wanted. We could have used hardware from the start."

Mr. DeLucca focused on Kartar and Kartar's hands curled into fists. Noah was making his move.

Kartar said, "Well, Noah, is now the time to lay blame?"

Noah shrugged. "I'm just saying—"

"The Winner needs to be driven from the server or we are going to have problems."

Noah seemed willing to open that can of worms, so Kartar mentally reviewed the decisions and the disagreements with Noah about Winner architecture. He'd always resisted Noah's control of the Winner, where easygoing Donny let Noah dictate everything on the system's back end.

"You're saying my thick client design would have problems. Could you run those past me again?" Noah said. He had the nerve to say this relaxed and cross–legged, as if he'd forgotten the hallway shouting matches after each presentation Wow had put together.

Kartar looked down at Noah. "Do we really need to go over this again? It's all in the architecture document," he said, stalling in order to search email for key discussions.

Noah looked pained and took out his iPhone.

Kartar found them on the subject 'Whose dumb idea was this?' started, of course, by Noah.

Noah still flicked his phone when Kartar leveled his at Noah and began recapping points.

". . . AND—excuse me Noah—and starting costs: purchasing a large number of simple thin clients is cheaper than more powerful thick clients. Guests will lose or break Winners so the hardware has to be cheap; more O&M savings."

Noah didn't nod, but said, "Granted the last one could be true. But hardware is getting cheaper and faster all the time."

Kartar dropped his hands to his side. "Here comes Moore's Law again."

Donny looked at his watch. "Ah, guys? Look what time it is. I've a design review to attend in two minutes."

Kartar and Noah both nodded and admitted they needed to be there too.

Mr. DeLucca gave Noah a hand up. "That leaves us with your generous offer. Get whoever it is prepped for travel."

Noah's confusion faded as he remembered what he'd promised during the meeting.

Mr. DeLucca said, "Before five, I'll have a ticket ready for tonight's last flight out."

Noah's eyes widened as he left, too distracted to bother with the strand of hair hanging across his nose.

"Kartar, stay a moment. I want to talk to you," DeLucca said.

Kartar didn't appreciate the scary eyes Donny made as he passed by. Maybe Donny was screwing around, or maybe he was serious. Either way, it wasn't a cool thing to do. Calm down, Kartar told himself. But the bad feeling in his belly wouldn't leave for a number of reasons: the economy wasn't good, he had child support payments to make, and Dharma started college in two years.

Kartar pinched the ring hanging beneath his shirt. No matter what it took, he'd make this project great.

DeLucca started talking as soon as the door closed.

"Kartar, I worry about you."

Kartar, mouth opened, but didn't know what to say. He squeezed the ring tighter.

"And you should be worried too. There are people looking for someone to hold accountable. They tell me things and I say: Hold on. I hire great people. They may fuck up sometimes, but they're the best.

"But these money people .... They're not always satisfied with that. They only use the Gantt chart to see whose line is longest, and today they see team Wow and ask 'Who's the manager?' "

"But that's as arbitrary as a game of hot potato!" said Kartar. "Of course all the tests go through the GUI—"

"Are you doing your best?" DeLucca said.

Kartar nodded.

From a drawer, DeLucca removed something like a modem, except he didn't hook his computer to it. He switched the line leading into his phone to connect into the box and then connected another line leaving the box into the phone.

DeLucca talked while connecting cables. "Soon I'll have a phone conference with them and that's what I tell them. These people . . . they aren't patient. My suggestion is that, from now on, your line shouldn't be the longest. Then they'll see you're doing your best."

DeLucca opened the door for Kartar. "OK?"

Kartar nodded as he left. In the hallway, although he stood still, he felt as if he was moving, like his body was accelerating forward at a lightning pace. String theory, he thought. The universe is made of strings of energy. Maybe the strings that make me are vibrating at the wrong frequency. Lately, he'd felt more like a piano string being stretched out of tune.

A young man walked past and entered DeLucca's office with a new picture frame; then Kartar was at his desk, not at all remembering the long ride down in the elevator to the IT department on sub–level four.

What happened? He blinked, dazed, and looked around the office. The floor was too quiet. He was alone. Where was Donny and Noah?

"Oh hell!" The meeting! He rushed to the meeting room on another floor, feeling tired and ill after sprinting up stairs.

It felt like he'd spent a lifetime in meetings. Since Design Complete was months ago, every change meant they had to review it. Changing anything at this point was expensive. It was a six–step Waterfall, and as DeLucca had said, they were in the Test Phase—step four, but they still implemented functionality to new business requirements, steps one through three.

After the meeting, he didn't feel better. He told his developers he was going home. While getting his sunglasses from his desk, Donny waved him over.

"Hey Donny, I'm headed home. It won't do the project any good if I get the team sick."

"You look like hell."

Kartar nodded and started to leave.

"It was that talk with DeLucca, wasn't it?"

Kartar didn't know what to say.

Donny rocked back in his chair. "I don't know how to take that Godfather talk. It's not the wild Vegas '80s anymore."

Kartar said, "I have to go."

"Wouldn't it be something if your car exploded when you started it?"

Kartar didn't smile back. Donny's smile slipped off.

"Hey! The Old Man really got to you. You parked in Casino parking right? Well then, you're fine. Blowing up your car would damage casino property and scare guests away. The Old Man wouldn't let anything happen that was bad for business."

Kartar shook his head, wishing Donny would stop.

Donny rummaged through a desk drawer. "I've something that'll make you feel better." Donny palmed something but changed his mind before handing it over.

"No. A man in your condition needs something stronger. . . . Here."

Kartar peered in the drawer. Donny wrapped a magazine around something and handed it over.

"Return it after you get your own. There's no waiting period in Nevada, though you'll want to get a concealed weapons permit a.s.a.p. As you're an employee, you'll never get shook down by security, but a permit'll keep the police happy in between here and home."

Kartar unfolded the magazine and almost dropped the contents—a revolver. "What? What's this?"

"You know damn well what that is." Donny glanced if anyone was nearby. "A Smith and Wesson fifty cal. magnum, the biggest production handgun made. See those slots cut into the end of the barrel? They vent the discharge so it don't kick outta your hand."

"You brought this into work?"

"It's a casino, not an airport. Just keep it concealed and act civilized."

Donny showed how to cock the hammer back and ease it to 'safety.' The revolver looked the right size for a big guy, but the weight of life or death felt too heavy in Kartar's hand.

Donny said, "Don't look so worried. The loads are two–fifty grain, not such a big kick. Besides, any idiot can use a gun. Just like in the movies, point and shoot. Now go home and get some rest. You'll feel better with that within reach."

"I don't want it!"

"See? Working already! You're back to your argumentative self. Now scoot! Go home. Recover from your flu. Take it! I won't take 'no' for an answer."

#

Kartar drove into the late afternoon sun leaving the deep bowel of the casino parking garage. He paused at street entrance, blinking until eyes adjusted to the light. On the passenger seat lay the magazine, Data Architect Today, wrapped around the revolver. Though it was late in the day and hadn't eaten lunch, he didn't feel hungry.

He got off the Strip and onto the interstate. His heart raced at each ad–wrapped van sighting. Stress evaporated only after witnessing the absence of the nude woman in a top hat. Those high school punks. Could their parents be so strapped for cash, they'd pimp their car and kids out to advertisers?

He reflected on his own parenting, and on how good a kid Dharma was. Divorced a year, and this was the first summer he'd had her. Maybe she was bored while he was at work, or maybe she really was satisfied relaxing at home, reading books, and playing video games. Could looking after her really be that simple?

He drove twenty over the limit on I–215. Traffic was light. The sky above was as blue as the ocean in an ad for the Caribbean, and in opposition was the desert, creating a blinding sun of bleached browns and golds. Boulders surrounded by sand struggled for survival, looking worn and tired. Before his eyes, they were being beat down by heat and time into their basic components. Like them, stress would eventually erode him into granules of skin and bone. In the Test Phase, and yet, still changing the requirements, changing the design, and developing more code. Everything but testing! It's just a bad day, he told himself. He still had time. Tomorrow and the next day and the next. . . . He'd make the Winner succeed.

His phone rang with Darth Vader's theme.

"Mom?" Kartar answered.

"It's done my baby. It is done!"

"What's done?" There was weird chanting in the background. "Ma, where are you?"

"I warned you over and over not to divorce, Kartar. So much bad karma lies on your doorstep. My nightmares have turned for the worse."

Dad's voice broke in. "You're scaring the boy because you keep eating all that junk at night—"

"Stop or by Shiva, you'll fly back alone."

He couldn't believe what he heard. "Ma? You're back in India?"

"I found the best holy man in Tibet. He's a real Rishi and he can help you."

Dad's voice came from the background. "A real Rishi she says. More like really expensive—"

"Listen to him," Mom said.

Kartar, confused for a moment, decided she meant the holy man.

Dad said, "Yeah, he'll talk to you in your dreams . . . by spamming your email—"

Kartar set down the phone as his parents fought. Suddenly the car in front swerved away from the shoulder. An old, wrinkled Indian man wearing brown Carhartts coveralls sat full lotus on the white line, one hand raised with thumb out to hitch a ride, his eyes locked on Kartar's.

"The hell!" He swerved from the man. Eyes glued to the rearview mirror, he watched him raise a toast with a clay cup, the kind the chai wallahs used in India.

Something slammed into his car. He tried to stay in control but the guard rail—For a moment, only a wheel hung over the edge, then his world, his car, and his self became airborne.

He held his breath as Data Architect Today floated next to his head, as the sky and mountains changed places —the sky now beside dashboard instead of roof. Then impact: sand beating against the windshield, the car skidding across desert on its roof until stopping abruptly, its nose tipping forward and delicately touching the ground.

He gripped the wheel, confused as to which way was up. Something tapped against his forehead—his ring swinging from its chain. His collar–bone forced against shoulder–belt, his butt not touching seat. Outside, the desert floor was the sky. A roadrunner the size of his a hand dashed past the windshield and Kartar reflexively honked as to warn it from the road. The little bugger stopped outside the door for a moment and then ran to the rear. Through the side–view mirror, he watched the little guy dash away until a van laboring across the desert came to view. Kartar fished his phone from his pocket in a panic. It slipped from hand to roof, sliding to a stop against the sun visor. The revolver lay hooked around the rearview mirror, among pens, empty venti cups, and a floor matt.

He grabbed the phone and dialed 911 as the van slowly approached, its left side dented. Instead of a nude lady, the van had a headshot of a blue man from the Blue Man Group. They ran him off the road? The same people? Why? How did they find me?

The 911 dispatcher answered while he watched the van pull to a stop behind his car.

"I've been forced off I–215 and need the police before I get shot."

The voice from 911 kept asking questions. He wondered what Dharma would do when he never came home. 911 recorded everything. There would be tapes.

"Dharma, I love you."

"Sir? What location are you at? Are you on fire?"

He remembered how the roadrunner was out here alone and how it had made a break for it. He was alone too. He couldn't wait for 911.

He released the seatbelt and fell to the roof. The revolver was cold and heavy as he picked it up. He got the door opened and crawled out. At his feet was a plastic box the size of a D battery. He toed the box, revealing it had an antenna.

"A tracking device?" What the hell was going on?!?

The van stayed where it was, its occupants waiting for his next move.

He took off running for the interstate. The van sat idling until he had gone five car lengths, then spun around and gave chase. The engine roar filled his ears; adrenalized fear coursed through him. His legs moved faster than he thought them capable.

He waved the gun at the van while running, but it didn't make them stop. Closer, closer it came, the smell of coolant and oil growing stronger. Kartar kept running. They wouldn't leave him alone. They were such bad people.

He gripped the gun tight, and while running, swung his arm to point behind him and pulled the trigger. The pistol butt kicked his palm, inciting stings of pain that competed with the shock ringing in his ears. The van hesitated for a brief moment, as if the driver's foot had slipped off the accelerator, then surged forward again, like pedal was pressed to the floor.

Kartar turned again, now running sideways to aim. The van was nearly on him. He fired and steam plumed from the radiator. Kartar dove to the side and the van passed by; the blue man watched with large white pupils, as if shocked Kartar still lived. The van slid to a stop and immediately, doors opened and out poured people and

Irish step music; Lord of Dance again. The driver wore a leather pencil skirt and a formfitting black jacket. The passenger, the blonde woman from the morning, wore an odd, European hat, giving her the profile of a bird perched on her head. Both wore large Paris Hilton–esque sunglasses and carried handguns with much longer barrels than Kartar's—silencers.

He got up from the ground. "Who are you? What do you want?"

The two stood behind the front of the van and conversed in calm tones, their faces obscured by the steam pouring from the engine compartment.

He gripped the ring which still hung outside his shirt and wished the earth would just swallow him, take him anywhere but here.

Still squeezing the ring, he said, "I'm dropping the gun. Whatever you want, it's yours."

The driver leaned against the hood, steam billowing around her, obscuring her.

"We're here to deliver something to you. A Gantt chart," the woman with the hat said.

Kartar twisted the ring on its chain. "You mean DeLucca—"

Something disturbed the steam near the driver and his knee gave out from under him. Rolling onto his back, legs in the air, he squeezed the bleeding joint with both hands and screamed in agony. Something inside burned like a hot iron. He dug his thumbs into the wound, pushing past skin and tissue for whatever it was, but couldn't reach it.

A blood stain bloomed red down his pant leg.

"Why—"

His other knee exploded into a red mess.

His scream echoed over the sound of interstate traffic and the stepping beat of Lord of the Dance. No sound of gunfire.

"Why?" he shouted, falling to his back, praying help would arrive before he died. Before his eyes, the sky dimmed to a darker blue. Blood flecked his shirt and some was on his face. The bleeding seemed to slow and both knees suddenly stopped hurting. The end felt near. The necklace lay broken across his chest. The ring, missing. He lifted his head searching for the gun or ring —nowhere. Terror faded with shock and certainty of death. What was left was anger: this happened because DeLucca didn't understand software. While the women retrieved something from the van, Kartar pleaded with them, screaming that projects running late were common. The sky flickered between bright and dim like a bad florescent light.

"My–my ring. Where is it?"

The women approached, keeping their distance from each other so he couldn't simultaneously focus on both. They moved with the confidence of professionals, convinced they'd finish this job as certainly as the rising sun changes darkness to light.

He combed his fingers through sun–bleached dirt, but found no ring. The sun battered bright heat downward. Eyelids kept closing. Exposed skin, his face, his arms, hot all over. When the footsteps got close, the dry dusty smell of the desert blended with sandalwood and vanilla. Couture.

The one with the hat held a sheaf of papers in a gloved hand. She cast them into the air above so that they wafted atop him like autumn leaves, concealing him from the sun's rays. He lifted his head to look and though it took a while, his eyes finally focused enough to recognize the black lines and red squiggles: the Gantt chart.

"You don't need to do this. Noah! He threw me under the bus, didn't he! This is a mistake! This project will hit it big. The Winner'll release, I swear it!"

"That's rich," scoffed the woman with the hat. "Even my worst didn't come in over fifty percent late."

"You—you're a project manager?" Kartar said, more baffled than ever.

"Retired. Thank God," she said smiling while raising her semi–auto pistol.

The driver tisked. "Sis was a kinda grand poo–bah, weren't ya dear?" The driver's wavy locks were plastered tight to her head.

"Yes. A certified PMI trainer," Sis said and took aim. "A high priestess of the institute."

"Then you have to know. You must understand. We followed best practices. We had requirements and sign–offs, but change requests kept coming, and the directors kept allowing it!"

Sis feigned a yawn. "Yeah. I got out of that racket. It's tiresome working with people who want process and order, but are always breaking it. It's a business for sadists and masochists, and I know which you are." She toed his knee and Kartar cried out.

The driver squatted, her shadow sheltering Kartar's face from the sun. Her white skin severely contrasted with her black hair, a natural goth. "Don't ye be in a pair of cuffs when she enters ye bedroom." She patted Sis's leg which softened Sis's frown. "Kartar, you married dearie?"

"M–My ring."

A kind look came over the driver's face and she squatted down and lifted it from the dirt.

"This bit is whatcha looking? Why don't you wear it on your hand all proper now?" Her own was decorated with plain silver rings on all but her wedding finger.

Sis lowered her gun and lifted the hat brim higher. "Lex? What are you doing?" Her left hand too had the same rings.

Kartar sensed an opportunity to survive. "I'm divorced. She left me for an iPhone engineer. That's why the Winner'll be great. Must be great! I want her to be sorry. I've more at stake than money. I have pride."

He reached for the ring but she pulled back and smiled.

Kartar frowned, unsure if it was a smile or sneer.

"I'll call her when I make the cover of Wired; they'll do a feature on the Winner."

The driver, Lex, shook her head. "You're so fierce about this bit–o–gold that I reckon it's your totem." She leaned over, shadowing his face while studying him. Her eyes visible through sunglasses, looking into his, searching for something. "'Tis certain you'll take this with you then."

Tears trickled from his eyes while he thanked the gods. Finally she realized he was just a geek, mixed up in something bad and undeserving of death.

When he opened his mouth to say thank you, she dropped the wedding band down his throat. He choked and struggled not to swallow. She leaned over, held his chin, her mouth close to his, her lips pursed. She kissed the air between their lips and then stood, aimed her pistol, and both women fired: Lex put a bullet through his heart, and Sis shot Kartar in the head.

As brain activity faded into darkness, Kartar's last thoughts were of his daughter.

ROWING OVER A BETTER
WATERFALL

Requirements Phase →
　　Design Phase →
　　Development Phase →
　　　　Testing Phase →
　　　　Deployment Phase →
　　　　River of Glory and Riches

Kartar couldn't breathe, couldn't see, and could hardly move. He twisted, kicked, and discovered he could push himself up. A pillow lay on the bed between his arms and hands. He stared at it, shaking. A dollop of sweat slide down his forehead to the bridge of his nose. The pillow was soaked. The AC must've broke. Brightness from outside shinned through the window and beat his eyes closed again.

He felt sick, like he'd ate too much then climbed a

flight of stairs. Flipping the pillow to the other side, he lay back down, and calmed himself, thankful for not being dead and willing the dream to never return.

Must be the karma Ma kept warning him about. She had wanted to find him a 'nice wife,' i.e., an Indian woman. But Lisa was tall, bossy, and American, with eyes bluer than anything to ever come out of Gujrati, his parent's home state. She had been irresistible, while Mom's advice was antiquated. Now he was divorced, and although it was she who had wanted out, he had bad karma to deal with.

He sat up but couldn't straighten his neck, his wedding band and chain hooked a pajama button. He freed it and held the band before an eye, using it as a peephole. For a moment, the bedroom was unrecognizable. Desk and dresser were bare, missing Robin Williams books on Web Interface Design and Proceedings of the ACM on Computer–Human Interaction. They were stacked on the floor with his others:Code Complete, The Art of Navigating Waterfall Projects volumes one through three, and a box containing Testing the World with Record–n–Playback and Great Software Starts with Great Coding Standards volumes one and two, their spines visible in the box's mouth.

He dropped the ring, rubbed eyes, and slowly opened them again. His eyes weren't tricking him. His orderly bedroom was a mess of boxes.

"Dharma?" He entered the hall. Her door stood open and her room empty of everything but a bare bed and dresser. "Dharma?" he called out again, this time more urgently. He searched the kitchen, living room, and the rest. The place looked the same as the day he'd moved in. Everything but the furniture it came with was packed in boxes.

Someone must have done this while he slept. But

why? To get on some "Stupendous Gags" website? And more importantly, who? Noah, to get even for their fight in front of Mr. DeLucca? Donny maybe? And had he really dreamt that Donny had given him a hand cannon?

In the center of the living room he squatted, surrounded by boxes, a flat screen TV, and disconnected A/V equipment. Whoever it was, they'd be found and made to put this mess back in order.

He returned to his bedside table and found his old gomera green BlackBerry instead of the newer, state–of–the–art chrome one. Although email was in–synch, the newest messages were a year old: new job benefit info, original requirements, budget allocations, discussions concerning team size.

Where was Dharma? Kartar rang her but went straight to voice mail. He texted, 'Dharma, are you OK? What's going? Tell me where you are.'

A reminder popped up: Winner Requirements Complete meeting in thirty minutes. Lovely! Badgered about a meeting from project start—his, Donny's, and Noah's first day on the job, when they had reviewed the 'completed' requirements. The meeting was the culmination of three months of requirements gathering by directors and their business analysts. As they neared Requirements Complete, they recruited developers and then, finally, project managers. Just like him, Donny and Noah wanted the project because high–profile casino plus state–of–the–art handheld equaled glory that worked both as credit for stock shares and the possibility of switching to an even better job.

If he could attend that meeting today, things would be different. With his knowledge and experience of which requirements kept changing, he could adjust the course of the project and actually release on time.

Kartar un–boxed some clothes and got ready for work.

In the garage, more boxes sat piled around a car that looked suspiciously like the rental he had when moving in.

A broom leaned against the wall; with a violent kick, he sent it bouncing off the car door.

"They're going to put all this back." At work, the guilty would reveal themselves. He tried his daughter again as he got into the car. Dharma still didn't pick up. The key from his bedstead started the car and the tune of *I got you babe* played on the radio.

He drove from his neighborhood humming to Sunny and Cher. Sitting next to the freeway on–ramp was the Indian man from the nightmare, beard wagging vigorously in the wind and hand gesticulating for attention. Wind stole away whatever words he shouted. Godman colors covered his head: lines of canary yellow spanned forehead like an automobile grille, black hair pulled back and streaked with white, steel–blue painted sideburns framed his face. He stumbled forward in brown Carhartts and sandals, resembling some kind of Transformer mechanic who'd been added into a Bollywood movie.

Kartar wanted none of this. When the man blocked the way, Kartar swerved around him and continued onto the interstate, a chilly feeling descending into his stomach as he pushed the pedal to the floor.

#

The first thing Kartar did upon entering the building was go to his cubicle. Empty. Not even a desk. What was even stranger was that many cubicles were empty, even Donny's and Noah's. His BlackBerry nagged that he was late.

"OK, OK, have it your way." A quick detour for a

latte, but the coffee stand was gone: no coffee bar and no back wall full of kitschy Sci–Fi posters. He stared at the barren hallway in front of the elevator. Something was really wrong.

He entered the meeting room, hoping Donny would laugh at the joke they'd played and recount how they went through so much trouble, but everyone was all business at the long mahogany table. In black pants and T–shirt that said, 'Cthulhu for President,' was Noah.

Kartar felt angry so he just stood at the front of the room and watched them for tells that they were in on a gag. But saw nothing other than his coworkers giving him strange looks.

"Noah," Kartar said. "Who won the trip to India?"

"Huh?" Noah looked confused.

"Here's our new wheel of project management," Donny said with a wink. "I guess that makes you the third wheel."

Theckla laughed, her pen inking a Richter scale of joviality across a document. LG just grinned, a red and a black pen held ready in each hand, ambidextrous; two more pens poking from her curly Irish–red hair.

LG looked at her watch. "Glad you could make it in Kartar. We hope to finalize requirements today."

"Sorry I'm late," Kartar apologized, but felt he shouldn't have to, since he was the victim. It was long past time they copped to the joke. He stood, watching but only got more puzzled looks from everyone except LG. Hers was a dead stare, the kind given to those not measuring up, as if she'd forgotten all the favors he'd done, such as accepting her never–ending outpour of requirement changes.

Kartar said, "We are finalizing requirements? Again?"

LG rolled her eyes. "Have a seat. We've a lot to do." The group turned away from him and went back to discussing the document.

Kartar, now thoroughly confused, sank into the chair beside Donny, because if anyone would cave and announce the joke was over, it would be him, a big man with an even bigger heart.

Theckla, her blonde hair now bobbed again, as it had been a year ago, said, "I'm glad you're here Kartar. LG wanted to know how many screens we'll need to process the user's credit card."

Kartar blinked a few times before speaking, and dried his sweaty palms on his trousers. "But we decided not to do that."

Theckla and LG looked at each other, puzzled. LG tilted her head and cupped her ear as if mishearing. Theckla popped her gum, the sound cracking the silence, then centered eyes on him through horned–rimmed glasses. "Have you been holding meetings without your business analyst?" Her voice, pitched low like she said something scandalous; an eyebrow arched above the frames of her glasses. Although her expression was almost comical, she was completely serious.

"Well—no!," his face warming under her steady gaze. "Remember, we're going with Visa."

The analysts looked at each other again. Theckla shook her head. "What are you talking about?"

LG set her hand on Theckla's. "Hold on." She pointed a pen at Kartar. "There are several problems rearing their heads right now. 'We' decided not to process credit cards? A, how are guests supposed to buy electronic chips, and B, who is the 'we' that decided to change the requirements without the presence of an analyst?"

They waited for an explanation while Kartar thumbed his phone for the email. "Theckla, you can't tell me you don't remember. We spent a month building the screens and Donny's team developed data models, and before it was finished, the Casino decided to enter into a partnership with Visa where Visa handles everything with their system. We just pass an authentication token between our systems and . . ."

Theckla pulled off her glasses and tapped ear piece against her teeth. "Now I feel like I'm the one late to a meeting."

Noah stopped twisting his hair. "As Chief Architect, someone should have told me about Winner coordinating with a third party system."

Every face around the table focused on Kartar and none were happy: Theckla looked betrayed, Noah and LG angry, and Donny puzzled. The confusion was palpable, and yet, unbelievable, as it all had been implemented months ago.

"I'll forward to LG—," said Kartar, and then at Donny's look, "I'll forward the email to all of you. It came down through DeLucca."

Kartar thumbed the scroll–ball while everyone watched and waited, until he eventually gave up in disgust. "My damn phone thinks it's last year."

Donny glanced at the phone's screen for a moment. "What are you talking about? That's today's date." Donny patted Kartar's back, "But don't let me stop you from dragging the Casino kicking and screaming into the future."

"What are you talking about? I don't understand."

Noah said with real compassion, "You just need a latte because you're still on Bay Area time. Don't worry. You'll adjust."

LG stopped gaping at Kartar, turned back to the papers in her hand and said, "I want to get these finished today and get Director sign–off. So I'll just put your team down for delivery of twelve screens."

Kartar shook his head. "It can be done in three, but

I'm telling you—we don't need any at all."

Everyone stared.

"Pad your estimates a little," LG said. "As far as the Casino is concerned, it all needs to be done in a year anyhow, so I don't care how many screens you need."

He gave up objecting, sitting there baffled as the group moved on to the next requirement. He drummed fingers on the document before him and immediately saw the problem—its revision date was a year old. He looked back up. Donny and Noah both were animatedly discussing the project, trading comments with Theckla and LG. Everyone was earnestly working on year old documents. It couldn't be an act.

Sweat dripped down armpits, heat spread down his neck. His heart was racing. Was he going crazy?

A text from Dharma arrived, jarring him from his stupor: 'No I'm not OK. You just left! Why didn't you tell me you were going to move?'

He put his hand over his mouth, wondering how could this be. Why would she say this? Why now? After the divorce, he'd decided overnight to take the Vegas job, leaving the Bay Area that morning. But that was old news. Much had changed since then.

Something phenomenal had clearly happened; everything was wrong, up–side down, ass–backwards. And it couldn't be a joke. What was happening was too comprehensive to be practical: re–packing the house, switching his car, switching phones. Dharma's text.

He was caught in some absurd time–warp. He was re–living the start of the Winner.

The meeting intruded retrospection. Silent, he watched them discuss the location of De'Arte's brand on the UI. This simple detail had caused a month's worth of work: redoing layout, requesting sign–off that the requirement had been satisfied, not getting it, redoing layout again.

The directors couldn't decide until Douglas, the directory of marketing, persuaded the rest to add a marquee with the logo at the top.

A delicious idea came to Kartar: Tell them what they want before they even knew it. He could fix the project's problems. It'd be easy the second time around. In many ways, this was a project manager's dream, an unprecedented chance to run a project the right way, from the start. Having already a year of experience, he'd be the most qualified person on the project.

The room quieted when he stood and walked to the whiteboard. He sketched a quick example and they quickly accepted the idea. Energized, he took control for the next requirement, and the next. He filled the whiteboard, he used pens and paper, he pushed ideas, suggestions, and influenced requirements closer to what they'd discover in the next twelve months. As the meeting continued, issues started to appear.

LG began to push back, crying out the requirements were already complete, that, "They're set in stone and Development should never presume to change them." Noah was upset and said, "You're going too far with your team building their own GUI architecture. It needs governance as part of the architecture's common set of services."

Kartar said, "If we need to have every GUI design change go through you, it'll just slow us down. We often didn't know what we needed until we needed to build it."

Theckla looked at LG. "He said that in past tense." Then looked at Kartar. "Maybe you meant to use subjunctive—"

"Hold on Kartar," said Noah, and the conversation got louder and louder, voices battling with one another for dominance. Donny rocked back, last year's sunglasses with the rose tint slipping down his sweaty forehead to land on his nose.

Donny said, "Kartar, you need to slow down, back up a bit. You're mixing design and requirements together. Don't worry. We'll start the Design Phase as soon as we're sure that the requirements are complete and that it's doable in a year. We can even start the Design Phase tomorrow, if today we decide the requirements are complete."

"But I already know they aren't complete," Kartar replied.

Theckla and LG set their pens down. Noah chewed his lip and Donny's elbows pressed onto the table, face resting in palms. Silence.

Kartar clicked the cap back on the whiteboard marker he held and returned it to the tray and sat heavily into his chair, pushing the documents before him to the side as the bright future of running the project the right way dimmed considerably. Was it possible that the future could already be 'set in stone?' Would he be able to change anything? And Dharma. . . . Oh gods, Dharma! She'd be away until next summer! Kartar frowned, thinking about the lonely first year after the divorce. Just a few days ago, he'd shown her how to mix milk and herbs for evening chai.

LG manufactured a smile as genuine as a Barbie doll's. "I can see we aren't going to reach agreement today. Let's take a break, cool our heads, and try again tomorrow. On a hopefully lighter topic, the Casino thought your teams would be more likely to get into the spirit of things if they had fun team names. That's what a Casino is for, right? Fun?"

While Donny and Noah looked thoughtful, Kartar leaned forward. "Wow. The GUI team will make the Winner an amazing experience. We'll be Wow."

"I adore it," said LG.

"Noah and the architecture team," said Donny. "Kinda

like a band. Maybe Noah and the Architects."

"Too long," Kartar and LG said at the same time.

"How about this," Kartar said, barely believing they were actually going through this again. "Noah's Arch."

"Love it!" said Noah.

"I knew you would," said Kartar.

LG said, "And what about the server side team?"

Donny's mouth opened, but Kartar quickly interjected, "Ka–Ching."

"That's exactly what I was thinking!" said Donny, his jaw hanging open, eyes wide with shock.

"Ya. I know," said Kartar.

The meeting finished with everyone smiling. Everyone but Kartar.

#

Kartar sat in his cubical while two people from facilities installed his desk. A short distance away, Donny and Noah moved into their own cubicles. Noah built a whiteboard city in his, whiteboards covering all four walls with two more rolling boards besides, already filled with scribbles and lines and comments regarding race–condition, transactional, often ending with the word 'WDIWT?' pronounced "wood eh wit" standing for 'Whose Dumb Idea Was This?' Donny mounted a small basketball hoop to his wall and searched for space to lay down a putting green.

While the two worked, LG stood in the aisle with her hands on her hips and making declarations like "Development's trying to take over," "It's the Casino's project," and "Who put Kartar in charge?"

It was hard to ignore her agitations. He needed a different tact. Warnings from science fiction movies sprung to mind. Could the future be changed, or was the path already determined?

He hadn't brought his personal effects into work like 'the last time.' That was a difference. The first time he'd experienced this day, he, Donny, and Noah had signed off on the Requirements and agreed they could deliver everything in twelve months. Another difference.

Although the Casino and the BAs had been working on the Requirements for months before hiring PMs, they weren't accurate. Last time, they had had a lot of problems. The Design Phase took over four months to complete. They finally declared an end to the Development Phase in June and started the Testing Phase, knowing full–well a lot of bugs were waiting for testers to find.

The Test Phase was where everything had come undone. India couldn't even get the application working well enough to do testing. And then killers clothed in designer labels marooned and murdered him.

He squinted as if there again, sun beating down, sheets of paper, the Gantt, covering him like a funeral shroud. Ghost pain throbbed in a knee.

One way to change the future would be to go to DeLucca and quit right now. Just walk away. Go back to LA, try to find a new project. But jobs, good jobs, were rare now. The divorce agreement was that she'd pay for Dharma's day–to–day needs and he'd pay for her education. Dharma was his life now. She needed to get into a great college, and that meant a lot of money. He'd leapt at this job, because it would be a rocket to financial security. Then there was the possibility that he'd be thrown under the bus when things went south. People say the first rat that jumps ship is the biggest rat.

So how to fix this project?

He pondered this as he stood, waiting for his desk to be finished and watching his colleagues. The requirements document was what killed him. Too vague. Had been from the start. The developers had to guess on most things, and those guesses meant time wasted on building wrong solutions before managing to create what the Casino had actually wanted. Too detailed at the same time. Or at least, the wrong details. Throughout the Design Phase, LG made had made change requests to adjust certain details. Then during the Development Phase, she filed bug reports that were actually change requests, because the software had followed details from the requirements. It was infuriating.

He brushed hand against his burly pompadour and thought about how slow and painful all of that had been. Couldn't really fault the Casino, because some of those details were unquestionably wrong. The truth was, they'd rushed into the Design Phase with lousy requirements—practically everything they'd planned was discovered to be wrong in a later phase.

A woman from facilities entered to set up his phone and workstation. She startled when he suddenly snapped fingers together—he'd ensure the Requirements were right from the beginning, and he already knew what needed changing!

He started to plan as he stood there, ignoring the technician until he almost forgot she was there. Get the GUI Architecture design document finished and reviewed within days instead of months, while getting the right requirements into LG's document at the same time. His team would simultaneously start their design documents as well. With both phases operating concurrently, they'd enter the Development Phase next month instead of four months from today. It would change everything!

Despite every reason to remain terrified of what had happened to him, Kartar felt better now that he had a plan and pushed thoughts of killers to the back of his mind where they weren't so vivid. This time around, he couldn't fail.

He sat at his workstation and typed with trembling hands meeting invites to his three developers, then worked on the GUI Architecture design document, each keystroke bringing him closer to a killer Winner project, to glory, and to getting Dharma into a great college . . . maybe even Stanford.

#

On the way to work, the crazy–looking mechanic sat in a lawn chair next to the on–ramp and waved the following sign at Kartar:

DOING THE SAME THING
+ EXPECTING A DIFFERENT RESULT
= INSANITY

When Kartar entered the conference room at last, the developers were scattered among the twenty leather executive chairs, as if to prevent a possible grenade blast from taking everyone out at once. Was it a bad sign they never sat close together? Rockstar, laptop closed, sunglasses on, one foot on the windowsill, mourned how much money he'd lost on horses. Kong sat at the other end of the table, laptop open, in a video conference with his mom and dad in Hong Kong. And from the tone of the Cantonese, Mom was upset at Dad again.

Prince sat in the center, eyes focused on his laptop screen, moonlighting as an editor for STRIP EXPOSED, some kind of literary magazine full of stripper stories and Casino poetry.

Kartar handed out a stapled document. "I made a draft of the GUI Architecture design document."

Rockstar said, "Oh? We haven't reached Requirements Complete, so it's too early for design documents. Today's supposed to be light. I'd planned on wagering on some races—"

"Yes, you're right. Normally we'd wait. But I've a clear idea of what the Casino wants. It's not all documented yet, but will be after a few weeks with LG. We'll do designs at the same time. I want you guys coding by next month."

Prince looked up from his editing. "I'd love to cut some code, but shouldn't we write this document together?"

"You guys are too important to bother with that, so I've already started. It's currently at 60 pages, so I suggest we start going over what I have."

Prince made a face and didn't close his laptop. Kong said "Bye," to his parents, his voice sounding like a disappointed child's, then poked at the papers that had been set in front of him.

Kartar said, "It'll be finalized after I run it by Noah." He set a different document in front of Kong. "This is the GUI Requirements for credit card processing. LG has made it more complicated than it needs to be. King Kong, I know you love model–view–controller, so please hammer out a design document for doing this in three screens while Prince, Rockstar, and I review the GUI architecture."

The team looked at him strangely. Only Rockstar flipped through a few pages, but then closed it, lifted it, and said, "It's got a good heft. I say we call it good."

Kartar brushed thumb down sideburn and focused on the bristle–sound the hairs made instead of getting mad. "And by the way, LG thought we should have team names, so we're called Wow." Kartar smiled again.

The team looked at each other then Prince slammed

his laptop shut. "What the hell? OK. I'm gonna ask."

Rockstar smiled. "You're the last one to fanny around."

Prince shot him a look and said, "Who's King Kong and these others you're referring to? The only people in the room are us."

Kartar's smile faded as he realized his mistake. They'd given each other these nicknames a few months into the project, after Rockstar ended up in jail for getting into a fight at a rock concert and Prince bailed him out wearing a Purple Rain T–shirt.

Rockstar tipped his sunglasses down and pointed at King Kong. "Since credit card payment requirements are in front of David—"

"And my surname is Kong," King Kong said.

Prince shook his head. "I can't believe what goes on in those management meetings." He leaned over the table and hung on to it with both hands as if it would jump away. "I'm guessing LG put in a requirement that David become 'King Kong.' I suppose she gave us all nicknames."

Kartar looked at the faces around the table. King Kong looked as if he didn't mind the nickname. Prince, however, still white–knuckled the table, and Rockstar's persistent smile looked pained. There was an easy way out. Kartar put hands into pockets, crossed fingers, and took it.

"Prince is right. LG's going to have IT change your email addresses to reflect your nicknames. You to Rockstar and you to Prince."

"I get 'Rockstar?' Brilliant!" Rockstar smiled and flipped open the GUI Architecture design document.

Prince opened a document as well, but shook his head. "My girlfriend has this horrid Purple Rain concert shirt she wears to bed. I wouldn't be caught dead in it."

"Purple Rain?" said King Kong.

"I'll send you a link," Kartar said. "Right now, we need to review these documents. Let's get halfway through by 6."

"There go the races," said Rockstar, pouting.

"What about you, Kartar?" Prince asked, chewing his lip. "What does LG call you?"

Kong said, "I see guys like him outside other casinos. But they wear a shiny white suit—"

Prince snapped fingers together. "Yeah!"

"It's blatantly obvious Kartar." Rockstar laughed. "You're our Indian Elvis."

Strange, thought Kartar, last time they were happy with just Kartar.

DEATH BY DOCUMENTATION

Waterfall Software Development Life Cycle — A process for creating software products with industrial–like precision. The Waterfall process has several variations, all of which have phases that are entered once and completed before entering the next, like water cascading down the steps of a waterfall.

Daily, Kartar toiled to usher co–workers up to speed: communicating with LG and DeLucca regarding requirements they'd yet to realize they wanted (and needed), persuading Noah to agree to his GUI architecture without spending months squabbling over particulars, and marshaling his team to adhere to documentation standards and coding conventions. June turned into July, then to August and then September, and Kartar was still laboring to get the Casino to agree to the requirements changes they'd wanted the first time around. So much time could be saved if everyone would just do what he asked!

And those were just his work problems. At home, he was forced to live his bleak, post–divorce life all over again: Ma, demanding a call twice a week; waiting the eternity to next year's summer school break, so Dharma could visit; and the iPhone, again, getting lots of positive press.

On bad days, he'd squeeze his ring until the band pressed into flesh a white circle—a symbol of infinity. No longer a marriage promise, but a vow to do whatever it took to be a success. A symbol of his resolution to fight day after day, month after month, challenging everyone to push the Winner to the next phase. The Winner would fix everything—Kartar Patel would be on the front cover of Wired instead of Steve Jobs.

Crazy mechanic reading Zen in the Art of Motorcycle Maintenance and a new sign propped against lawn chair:
    FIRST WEEK OF OCT.
    STILL REQUIREMENTS PHASE.
    WHEN STUCK IN INFINITY,
    LIBERATION THROUGH
    CHANGING UR LIFE

LG stood over Mr. Kong as he worked. "I don't care what Kartar told you—"

"You're the Casino Analyst. Kartar's my boss. I listen to the boss when two people tell me different things. Don't be upset—"

"Just follow the Requirements and don't be a monster."

"Ha, ha. King Kong. Funny. You know what? No one told me I was being called a big monkey. I figured it out when Prince said I should wear a monkey suit for Halloween—"

"That's great! Do you understand why we have Requirements? We use them to FOCUS development."

"If we just use a different selector, we could do this in two screens."

"Mr. Kong, because of your boss's overactive imagination, the Requirements are changing. A lot. It's better if you design to the Requirements because people are putting in overtime to get them right. I don't exactly recall why we wanted to do this in twelve screens, but I guarantee you, there was a reason. See these gift certificates for the new latte stand? I want to be involved as you document the design so I can make sure you understand what we want. I'm scheduling weekly meetings. When the meeting ends, I'll leave a handful of certificates on the table. I hope they are gone before the next meeting starts. Got it?"

Theckla leaned against the wall, listening to LG and King Kong. She was about to leave but noticed the tone in LG's voice. She shook her head and resumed her eavesdropping. When LG left Kong's cubicle, Theckla caught her attention.

"I heard you and King Kong. You're really doing some horse–trading. Do you really think all those screens are necessary? I remember we put twelve in the Requirements because we rushed Kartar through that meeting."

LG slipped a pen behind an ear. "Let me put it to you straight. I have thirteen years of experience on software projects, and sometimes I push for things that don't make sense today, but that I'll need for leverage later on. Maybe only a few screens are necessary as they keep saying, but I guarantee you that, before we go–live, the Casino will want more screens somewhere in this very complex application. Those extra screens are a savings account on the Gantt. When I give Wow a CR and they complain there's no time to do the work, I'll sweeten the deal by reducing the number of screens needed for CC processing." LG dusted her hands together. "Quid pro quo, and everyone's happy."

Theckla puckered as if tasting something sour. She started to leave, but hesitated when LG's mouth shaped into a smile as Rockstar passed.

LG said, "You know, I really enjoy the official tone Rockstar brings to meetings. It's like listening to a BBC report."

"That would be because he's British," Theckla said, then turned away, leaving.

It was morning and Rockstar was still feeling the effects of last night's Gun Shooting Knives performance at the Pepper Mill. He felt worn, 'slogging through London in rubbers full of water' worn. Prince entered his cubical and said, "King Kong's right behind me, and based on the unhappy look on his face, I think he needs help with CC processing. Catch a latte afterwards? That new stand just opened."

Rockstar stared while the words sank in.

Prince said, "Right. Afterwards."

"But I need one now!" whined Rockstar.

Kong crowded into Rockstar's cubicle.

"You're all his," Prince told Kong, vacating as quickly as he'd entered.

"You have no honor!" Rockstar shouted to Prince's back.

Kong made a face and clicked tongue to roof of

mouth.

"I'm still having trouble getting my CreditCardProcessor class working with your InfoBucket class."

"You're writing code?" said Rockstar, surprised.

"Yes."

"You're rather naughty, aren't you? We've not yet finished the Design Phase. It's October, and despite Elvis's promises, we still haven't finished the Requirements Phase."

"Kartar says after Requirements, we'll have a week to finish the Design Phase. He wants us to be ready. LG says after the Design Phase, change controls will be in place."

Rockstar threw his hands upward. "Change controls! But things are always changing! Change controls mean we waste time filling out paperwork."

"LG says design changes would need approval by the directors. How to explain design to people who don't use email?"

"Bollocks mate."

"I want to test my design by building a prototype on top of yours. You test it?"

"Kong! You're hurting my feelings now! I walked through those classes with the debugger. The code's golden!"

Kong rubbed at his face like his forehead and cheeks were stained by something to be wiped off. "I've been trying to get it working for two days. I don't see the problem."

"Two days? You should have asked for help earlier."

"Two days isn't much coding time. We have too many meetings and documents to review. Maybe only fifteen minutes a day."

"That's why I shuffle into work late and leave late, so

I've time to actually get something built. Email me the code you're using and I should be able to get to it tomorrow. As of now, I'm busy coding messaging infrastructure for the architecture. Noah will toss me off the Arch team if I don't finish."

Kong sat in his cubicle, staring at the CardProcessor class for the umpteenth time. There was definitely a problem somewhere. Just couldn't see it.

For a change of pace, he switched to email and started through the inbox. Email; an easy, work–related distraction to pass the time until an answer fell from the sky. The phone rang before he got through the first. Caller ID showed it was Kartar.

Kong knew what Kartar wanted. For the past ten minutes, he'd been ignoring a meeting reminder. Kong picked up the phone and before Kartar could say a word, said, "I have no time for meetings today. I need to work on some code. I'm having troubles."

"Theckla says you're not attending meetings because you're still working on CC processing's design document. Two months ago, you said it was finished."

"It was. But last week, LG told we'll have change controls after the Design Phase. So I need to test to make sure the design's right."

"Dammit Kong!" Kartar said. "CC processing's requirements don't matter! The whole thing'll be outsourced!

"Look . . . sorry I yelled. All we need is something quick to keep LG happy until everyone sees I'm right. Drop what you're doing, and help us review the GUI Architecture document. That's what's going to save our collective asses during the Development Phase. I want to try to finish the Design Phase in one day."

"A day! You said we'd have a week!" Kong sank low in his chair, back lying on the seat, head held forward by the chair back.

"Kong, I'd love to give you a week. But the Gantt shows it'll be a tight race to complete coding before the Test Phase. We'll gain another week if we review all the Design docs and call them complete at the end of the day."

Another sign:
2nd   WEEK OF OCT
STILL IN REQUIREMENTS PHASE?

While Kartar trolled through the day's hundred–or–so emails, Theckla suddenly appeared at his side as if there was a fire she was escaping. Or one she had started.

"Give me a sec," Kartar said, desperate to get through the logjam. "I'm reading your's right now."

Theckla didn't. "You know I'm your biggest fan. And it's not just because of those Elvis sideburns and that killer pompadour. Kartar, your team's been really busy. Busier than a one–legged men in a butt–kicking contest. I get they're writing design docs at the same time we're doing requirements docs, but there's a lot of code being written to get those designs finished. Isn't it too early to do development? Shouldn't your team wait until the Requirements Phase and Design Phase are finished? There're a lot of moving parts and having them all moving at the same time feels . . . calamitous."

The dark glasses Theckla wore today looked like teak but were made of many tiny cubes, so even the rounded parts appeared blocky. "Minecraft?," he asked.

Theckla blushed. "Found the model online. Burned a

bundle to buy the right filaments to print a teak pattern."

"Wow! Minecraft in hardwood!"

"The team! No docs!"

"Yes, about that. I'll ask them to focus on finishing documentation. Normally I'd worry about doing design while requirements are incomplete, but trust me Theckla, this time the requirements will be on the money. If there's a project which could do it, it's this one."

He had the inside track.

Kartar was almost through his inbox when LG arrived. "Just a second," he said, holding up a finger to keep her at bay a moment longer. She ignored it and pressed on as he knew she would.

"The Casino can't keep taking this Kartar! All of these new requirements just keep coming out of thin air."

Her head shook with violence, locks wiggling as would tightly wound springs. "Every time I release a doc for comment, you fill the margins with 'suggestions.' How do you know the Casino will ever want to change games? Why would the Casino want this 'Whack–a–Mole' game you call Whack–a–Dollar? The Casino wants one, not two, or three, or dozens, ONE, one simple electronic slot game. Is your name LG? No. I'm the one who talks to the Casino. I'm the lead analyst. A simple slots game, Kartar! That's what the casino wants, simple slots!"

Prince removed his shades and stared at the cover of the GUI Architecture document while scratching sunglasses against cheek stubble. The document read like it belonged to a different project. A lot of the design didn't match with the Requirements. Kartar kept saying that, soon, the

Requirements would match to their design and to trust him. Prince shook his head. Damn. He and the other developers would be the ones working the late nights to build it, not project managers and analysts.

Prince pushed the eighty–plus page document aside and called Rockstar. "Let's rap entertainer to entertainer. Why does Kartar have such a complicated design in section seven? Why can't this be done with a few simple classes instead of twenty or thirty?"

"Sorry mate. I gave up in section three. I'll save my eyes for something more rewarding, such as polishing ash bins. Kartar and Noah are bound to have a dust–up when we start the Development Phase. Let them battle it out and when they settle, we just do what they want."

"I'm going to talk to our Indian Elvis."

"Go ahead, but remember, the King trumps a prince anytime. So keep a stiff lip if it's a waste of time."

Kartar stood in Donny's cubicle, enacting an angry LG, pressing the backs of his hands against his head and waggling fingers to simulate her hair. "She barged into my cubicle, big 80's hair flying and crazy—yes Donny, I was born here. I saw those styles in LA at my parent's motel."

Kartar's hands lowered. "Who do you think had to vacuum hair off the floor when cleaning rooms? Anyway, you heard her. 'The Casino wants simple slots! The Casino wants simple slots!' When did she ever want simple anything?"

Donny shook his head. "She keeps saying, 'The Casino,' like she meets with some kind of ruling entity. Maybe it's Jabba?" Donny leaned close to Kartar, squinting, obviously searching for a tell.

Kartar shook his head. "Yes, I saw Star Wars too. Stop

testing me."

"Maybe she will settle for something simple."

"The day we finalize any documents of any kind—Requirements, Design, or Test Plans—on simple slots, she'll change the Requirements to add flashy graphics. We'll agree to that change and then she'll be back—during the Development Phase—asking for video. You take my word on that! LG, or the entity known as the Casino, won't settle for simple anything! You can take my word on that!"

DeLucca smiled as Noah entered his office and sat down. DeLucca stayed sitting behind his desk and said, "I get that we have three teams and need to split the work among them, but explain to me the difference between an architecture and a vertical. And make it easier to understand than one of your shirts. What the hell is 'No place like 127.0.0.1' supposed to mean anyway?"

Noah grinned. "127 dot zero dot zero dot one is the network address for home. So, no place like home." DeLucca still didn't appear to understand so Noah moved on. "So your question on architecture. Think of a building. No matter what purpose it serves, it needs plumbing, electricity, and phones. These common things are what my team builds. Donny and Kartar's part of the Winner are the verticals, meaning, those structures built on top of the architecture. Donny manages data. Kartar builds the games and develops the game experience. Both of those teams need the plumbing, electricity, and phones if they're to do their jobs correctly. If Kartar's team built their own plumbing, they would need to develop and debug it to see if it held water. And Donny would need to do the same thing. It's more efficient for the Arch team to build one set of plumbing and in a standard way, so that all teams benefit. It's just as vital as coding and debugging. And in the future, we can add more verticals that use the same architecture."

Sign:
SHOULDN'T IDEAS COME FROM ALL LEVELS?
FOCUSING ON ROLES AND HIERARCHY
SQUELCHES INNOVATION.

Donny was busy reading email so Kartar leaned over the cubicle wall in an effort to be less disruptive. "When LG comes up with a requirement, she glosses over the details. When I do, every little nuance needs to be explained, documented, and met over. What's up with that?"

"I'm not going to lie man. It's been hard understanding all those requirements you've been," Donny winked, "dumping on us." Donny raised his hands as if Kartar would leap to attack. "Her words not mine."

"I just want the project to go better." Kartar brushed a thumb down a long sideburn. His nightly rest was tormented by nightmares of being alone in the desert, fleeing the van. This time, it must go better. It had to.

"Heeeellooooo. . . . Who do you think those legs belong to?" Donny said, pointing with his chin. Kartar turned and got a glimpse of a tall woman striding away.

Donny sniffed the air. "Even turns the air beautiful."

The scent was familiar: partly vanilla and partly floral, delicate and expensive. Like one of the designer brands from the Bellagio that sold for over a thousand dollars. Kartar couldn't imagine who he knew wore it. It was too expensive to be something his ex had used.

Kartar said, "What were we discussing?"

"Have you heard that the directors will double our

staff? DeLucca's really taken to your requirements work, but doesn't think we'll get it done unless we staff up."

"Really? I'd only heard about the latest target for Requirements Complete as being Halloween. If LG wasn't so stubborn, we could've finished them months ago."

"If we're doubling staff, we're doubling costs. The Casino got a cash infusion from someone. I hear the investor wants to do audits."

"How do you hear these things? Your finger is on the Casino's pulse my friend."

"What I hear is your phone."

Kartar ran to his desk and picked up before it rang to voice mail.

"Kartar here."

"Kartar," said Prince. "I've a question about the GUI Architecture document. Could you come over?"

"Can we do this over the phone? I've an email to send to LG about our requirements."

"You have the doc in front of you? I've version twenty–three."

"The latest is twenty–six. You're outdated. I'll tell you what. I'll forward you the latest, finish my email, and be right over."

It had been a month since Kartar had visited the developer floor. Someone else now sat at Prince's cubicle and she informed him that Prince had been moved to a different location. Just as Donny had said, the casino was hiring more developers. He wandered around until he found Prince.

Kartar said, "Sorry. I didn't know you moved."

"The Arch team's taken over half the floor. They wanted my cubicle for a new guy. Keeping their team together as much as possible, I guess."

"Interesting." Kartar thought, why would the PM with

the shortest line in the Gantt staff up? Where was he getting the work that justified it? He looked at the document in hand and had a bad feeling.

Kartar said, "He's going to steal it from someone."

"What?"

That had to be it. An easy way to get more work was to take it from other teams. The directors' darling to the rescue, helping out poor struggling Wow and Ka–Ching. That had to be it: Noah planned to extend the architecture!

"Kartar?"

"Eh? Yes. What did you want to discuss?"

"Some of these classes look overly complicated. Your encryption module for instance—"

"I've spent a lot of time working on a design to support what our requirements will be. You and the team have reviewed my changes every week and you've never said anything until now. Let's have this discussion at next week's Design Review."

"We're doing all this before the Specifications have been completed. What if they change?"

"They won't. You, Rockstar, and Kong just need to build to the GUI architecture as designed."

Prince gave Rockstar a call. "I just talked to Kartar. He wants me to 'present my position' at the design review meeting."

"Congratulations! That's quite the incentive for your trouble! Good luck getting any words in edgewise with Kartar and Noah there. They're in diametric opposition, sort of an 'Elvis and Pope' situation."

"My prototype shows how to do this work more easily. But Kartar really loves his design. It's not worth the fight. Now, I'm with you. Let management do what they want and we'll just build those damn classes."

Crazed mechanic's sign:
   3rd WEEK OF OCT
   STILL IN REQ. PHASE?
   STILL DOING DOCUMENTATION?
   CONSIDER V1.0 > DOCUMENTATION,
   INCREMENTALLY DELIVER UR PRODUCT

Kartar stared at the team's documentation stacked on his desk. As project manager, he should review it all. After a deep sigh, he got to it and had finished flipping through nearly a hundred pages when his phone rang. The caller ID showed 'DeLucca,' so he picked up.

"Hello, Mr. DeLucca. No, I didn't tell LG I'm to be the source of requirements. She says that whenever I help fill in the details."

Kartar took a deep breath and thought about the Gantt chart the hitwomen had dumped over him: two bold parallel lines that represented Wow and Arch, and between, a blue line that bounced back and forth like a game of pong. The blue line moved from Wow to Arch whenever Wow gave Arch GUI requirements for the architecture capabilities they'd need to build the casino games. At that point, Wow was blocked from doing any meaningful work until the blue line traveled from Arch back to Wow, symbolizing a release of architectural features. However, Wow's bold line of work completed grew only a bit before discovering an additional requirement the GUI architecture lacked, so again they sent new requirements to Arch, the blue line traveling back with them, the Gantt documenting the game of hot–potato.

Arch complained Wow was ignorant because Wow's requirements had never documented all the necessary features. Wow complained Arch's releases took too long and were buggy, and as long as LG kept changing requirements, it was impossible for them to have complete requirements to give Arch the first time, the second time, the third time, and so on.

He'd be a dead man again if that blue line bounced too many times.

"Mr. DeLucca, I heard something the other day. Is Noah's team increasing head count? You know what I think we should do? Wow wants to help out. My team has tons of GUI expertise, and I was at Palm for all those years. GUI architecture work should be on Wow's plate. We're the ones using it to implement the games after all. I think we could knock it off quick, and heck, Rockstar's on the architecture team anyhow 17% of the time anyhow, so he's familiar with it. And Architecture's budget wouldn't need to keep growing to accommodate more head count. . . ."

Crazy mechanic's sign:
   OCTOBER ALMOST OVER
   STILL DOING REQUIREMENTS?
   WHAT'S MORE VALUABLE,
   DOCUMENTS OR SOFTWARE?

Kartar didn't like what Theckla reported when he chanced to run into her. Wanting to get to the bottom of it as soon as possible, he dashed back to his desk and made a call. "Kong? Are you at your desk? A little bird told me you're still working on CC Processing."

"Ahhh . . . maybe. LG told me directors want what's

in requirements, and I know she'll check that I have all eleven screens."

"What? The Gantt chart shows CC Design was finished in August. We're almost through October and you're still working on something I told you will be outsourced."

"Er—sorry. I wish people would make up their mind."

"____!"

"Kartar?"

"Sorry. Alright, how much time are we talking?"

"I don't want to say."

"I need to know so I can update the Gantt."

"The document is the size of your GUI Architecture design doc. I wrote a lot of code for the screens in CC Processing—twelve screens. I must prototype so I know the design is correct. LG and I meet every week. . . . Kartar?"

"I'm here."

"I thought we were cut off."

"October's almost over, and yet we're still finishing the Requirements Phase, and you've spent every day since June on CC processing. . . . This is terrible! We've a better Requirements doc now, but getting everyone to understand it is slowing everything down, and you're stuck doing the same thing you did last time!"

"Last time? What last time?"

"Never mind. You need to wrap this up today and I don't want to hear any more about CC processing."

Rockstar's phone rang. Kong—the fifth call of the day. "Yeah? That's what I'm bloody telling you, Kong. I tested it and it works fine on my computer. Have you got my most recent changes? Oh hell, I need to dash. Noah's headed towards my cubicle, fiddling with his hair scrunchie, and you know what that means."

Kartar sipped his morning chai and opened the GUI Architecture design document to make another revision. Even with all the knowledge he'd gained from the last time, he'd still discovered more refinements based on team feedback. He hadn't gotten far before Donny dropped by.

"Donny, it's too early for you to be here. I'm still waking—"

"You friggin' genius! You totally called it! LG was just at my cubicle, mad as hell, because she and Theckla just finalized CC processing design with King Kong and someone in Accounting sent her an email declaring a strategic agreement with Visa, and that Visa would be taking over all CC processing work. And get this—LG tossed that tome of hers onto my desk and it busted my phone!"

"Eighty pages, such a waste. I wanted it simple."

"Theckla said the directors will be signing off on the Requirements any hour now. What'cha looking through the online Yellow Pages for?"

"A Cadillac dealership. Have you noticed an ad–wrapped van in the garage lately?"

"Yeah! Jack's Halloween with the Rockettes. I wonder if ol' Nicholson can sing? Why do you ask? You have some kinda fetish?"

It was a 'morning' meeting at 10:00, and Prince and Rockstar sat at the table, flipping through Prince's design document as Kong arrived.

Prince said, "Look who's late to my review sporting bed hair!"

Kong's eyes flicked between Prince and Rockstar,

clothes looking rumpled and slept in, posture stooped.

Prince sighed at the stupefied look on his colleague's face. "No, it's not a rumor. Credit card processing's been outsourced."

Kong straightened, his hands on hips with fingertips pointing down, a slightly feminine effect.

"Me with LG spent so much time. Can't be!"

Prince patted Kong on the back, "Sorry man."

DeLucca addressed everyone at the Halloween Party. "Congratulations to everyone for their hard work on completing requirements for the Winner! It's amazing how it has evolved from what we thought we wanted in June to what we have now. We will revolutionize how people game. Because we believe so strongly in that, we've gone back for more funding and they've granted it. The investor doubled down on his bet and bought insurance too. A representative from Lovers Inc., an auditing firm our financiers insist we use, will be visiting on a regular basis. Please give them your full cooperation. Now, what we've all been waiting for, the winner of the costume contest is . . . Donny, as Flower Power Rambo! I don't think there's ever been so much tie–dye on someone who looked so dangerous."

Crazy mechanic's sign (there must be a security leak):
   FINALLY IN DESIGN PHASE!
   SO WHAT?
   5 MONTHS AND NOTHING SHIPPABLE.
   THE WORLD CHANGES,
   DOCUMENTS DON'T.

Kartar pinched the ring fiercely then turned around to face Thekla. "But I've had my team working on design documents since July."

"Mr. DeLucca was very clear. He doesn't want teams exiting the Design Phase early. He wants all three teams working in concert on one big, whole, happy project. It doesn't make sense to have the cake batter ready, but no pan built to bake it. And the auditors want the process followed. Have you met those two from Lovers Auditing? Both have the same last name. Maybe they're a package. Lex is nice, but Sis is clearly the brains of the outfit. And you can't miss them. The other day Sis was here in a pencil skirt, pin–stripe jacket, and expensive perfume— all very 'Ms. Business.' What's that look for? You've got something against pencil skirts? She must keep gold in that svelte clutch of hers. We were going over project documentation and her clutch was in the way. So I moved it aside and it was heavy as hell! And the look she gave me—there's an edge about her for sure. Donny's been giving her the smokey eyes."

Kartar recollected his latest nightmare: an ad–wrapped van pursuing him through the desert, the roadrunner running alongside and shouting encouraging words while he fired the fifty–caliber revolver at the van.

The revolver hadn't made a difference the last time, but at least it was something he could do. Something in his control.

Direct seemed the best approach so he entered Donny's cubicle and looked him straight in the eye. "Donny, I know you've a gun in your desk, and I want to borrow it."

Donny's eyes widened as if to deny it; then he relaxed and swiveled in his chair. "Kartar, although a handgun is effective personal protection, it's against casino policy to bring one to work—unless you have a good friend in Sec of course. Why would you need it anyway? Someone after you? Gambling debts?"

"I can't talk about it. Just lend it to me." Like last time, Donny rummaged through the bottom drawer, carefully wrapped it in a copy of SQL Database Professional, and handed it over.

"Thank y—This isn't it!" Kartar opened the magazine because whatever was inside wasn't heavy. "What's this? It's too small!"

"Isn't it though? The Colt Pinfire is the smallest production repeating revolver ever made, circa 1880. In Nevada, it's illegal to conceal without a license, but since it could fit in a bottle of ibuprofen, it's unlikely to be noticed. You break or lose it, you buy it plus a handling fee."

"But it's so small!"

"I'd worry about giving you something bigger until we talk some more."

"Hmmm. It'll do until I find something better. Hey, do me a favor and stay clear of that auditor. She's bad news. Trust me on this."

LG finally had Rockstar alone in a meeting room. The room was quiet, so silent, a passerby wouldn't realize it was occupied. He sat across the table from her, stiffly proper, his design document sitting squarely before him. She handed her requirements document to him, brushing his hand as he grasped it. Without a word, he went to work. He focused on his design document, she focused on his lips. How they pressed together and pouted while he studied her requirements, how they relaxed when he looked over his design, and how they softened into the barest smile whenever he drew a checkmark, confirming his design met the requirement.

Page by page he flipped through the docs and page by page the feeling of temperature of the room increased, until finally Rockstar broke the silence.

"Where are my manners! It's probably hard to see from there without a copy. Let me get one for you." He half stood up to leave the room.

"No, that's OK." She walked around the end of the table and sat beside him. "We can share. You're spending a lot of time on this item." She leaned close. "Is something confusing? I'd love to change it if it is . . . just so it's clear."

He sat, pressed lips tight together before opening them again to respond. "Well, why just Whack–a–Dollar? Why not whack five, ten, or twenty dollars? A dollar is hardly anything anymore, and the time it takes to write the code for a single dollar is nearly the same as it would be to design it to handle other denominations."

LG settled into the leather couch while George, Director of Casino Operations, looked over the document she had handed him.

"LG, I'm glad you brought this to my attention. Why whack singles? Why whack money at all? How about whacking drinks? Those are five to ten dollars in value, but only cost us one or two dollars to produce. Ask IT if the cost for implementing Whack–a–Drink is in alignment with the potential payback. If it is—"

She made a gun with her finger. "Fire off a change request." She cocked her thumb and fired.

Although Rockstar played every mental trick he knew to

keep composure, he flushed as soon as LG entered his cubicle wearing a skirt and perched herself on his desk, crossed legs in easy view.

"Don't be a tease Rockstar. How much more work would it be to do Whack–a–Drink instead of Whack–a–Dollar?"

"It is a lot more complicated than whacking different denominations. I need to look at this a bit."

"Oh, just give me a ballpark. No commitments. Between you and me—a secret. I promise."

"Ah . . . . Well . . . . Let me see . . . . Now the bar's point–of–sales equipment needs to be integrated into the Winner backend. That's really a bother. So . . . maybe Whack–a–Drink is an additional five engineering–months? That's just an off–the–cuff. Academic really, as there's no time to add anything more to the Winner. We shouldn't even be talking about new—"

Rockstar stopped talking because it was apparent she no longer listened. Her eyes fluttered upwards, springy hair a–wiggle, and lips moving as if having some sort of fit. She returned to normal when he stood to call for help.

"The Casino could save five to ten times more on costs per transaction with this instead of Whack–a–Dollar. The Casino requires this. I'll put in a change request."

Rockstar stared at LG, red hair bouncing while she strode away. "What—what have I done?"

The (mentally disturbed?) Indian's sign:
JAN 2ND
WHILE A SIGNED OFF DOC
WILL STAND IN PLACE,
A BUSINESS WON'T.

Theckla knocked on Kartar's cubicle and entered.

"Ah, my favorite BA."

"Your only BA. How did Christmas with your daughter go?"

Kartar looked embarrassed. "Had to cancel. Needed the time to catch up on documentation."

"You worked the whole holiday?"

Kartar said nothing.

"I see. . . . Are you ready for today?"

"Why? Something's happened!"

"I hope your GUI architecture is flexible because LG just documented a lot of requirement changes. Do you want to hear the easy or the hard first? OK, I'll pick. Whack–a–Dollar has become Whack–a–Drink."

"Hmmm. . . . A totally different system than we've had to integrate with before. What's the easy?"

"Ah, there's a new vertical for Casino Operations and an architecture section called Mood Management that requires a new piece of hardware: a front facing video camera."

"She can't do that! We finished the Requirements Phase two months ago. Hardware is being manufactured! We're finishing design this Friday and starting development Monday. This is completely out of process!"

"She swears the Casino must have these."

"We let in a change now, they'll want to do it again and again. The hardware vendor's going to pitch a fit!"

"Calm down. It's not as if an angel loses its wings each time this happens. It's just one last change."

Kartar took both hands and scrubbed them over his sideburns, then covered covered his eyes a moment, reviewing past project memories.

"No!" He stood.

"It will not be the last change! I'm finally getting it.

The Casino's like a five–year–old! Give in now and they'll only ask for more during Development and Testing."

"Come on! You're making a lot out of this. It's not that big of a deal."

"I'm telling you that last time LG started making change requests, she kept at it all through our Development and Test phases. One damn CR after another. For REQUIREMENTS!

"Last time? Did you two work together somewhere else?"

"This craziness must stop. Waterfall doesn't mean IT does whatever the Casino asks. They develop the Requirements and the rest is up to us. I worked too damn hard to make sure our Requirements had all the CRs she dropped at our feet last time we did this—"

"Last time? Kartar, what last time?"

"They shouldn't be asking for more."

"DeLucca wants this. He gave the CR its own name: Requirements 2.0."

"We haven't shipped 1.0 yet! Come! Let's go talk to DeLucca."

Theckla was rigid with stress, eyes blinking rapidly. "Take some deep breaths and slow down. I really don't think that's a good idea."

"We have to move fast. Come on!"

"An invitation to see Custer at his last stand? No–thank–you! You can tell me about it after the dust settles."

Kartar didn't like the color DeLucca's face became. His well maintained tan wasn't compatible at all with whatever was happening with his temper.

"I got to be president by taking the latest of what I see

and know, and making decisions based on that."

"But sir! The Requirements were declared complete! You, LG, and the entire board of directors signed–off at the Halloween party. Your signature's right here."

"Screw the signature! This is about killing the competition! Would you let a signature force you to execute on a bad plan? No! When you see an opportunity, you whack it over the head and take it. Mole, dollar, or drink!"

"We already have great requirements! They contain everything you could want!"

"Kartar, we kept going back to your changes as your insisted, and it took a while. . . . It took a hell of a lot of head scratching too, but now we're with you. We didn't realize how great the need was for deploying new games. We were only thinking of simple slots. Then Glenn got excited, saying your additions were like something out of his dreams, things that had bounced around in his head but he'd never fleshed out with LG. But you already had them in there!"

"Hmm, so those CRs during testing were Glenn's fault."

"What?"

"Nothing. So Glenn liked it."

"No, he loved it! He badgered the directors to figure out what we'd do with it. I mean the Winner's the bomb! Our bomb! We won't get another chance at this."

Kartar said flatly, "So the requirements I added inspired this Mood Management."

"I'm surprised you aren't happy. These changes are built from requirements you've been pushing. These new advancements, like adding the video camera, will make a splash like—"

"They're going to make design changes across the whole project. I don't see how we can do this within our schedule."

DeLucca shook his head. "We're still inside Design. That's what this phase is all about—changing things, searching for the best design."

"Because we finished most of our design work in November, we've been developing prototypes which will turn into our eventual product. But these changes, well, the guys will end up tossing a lot of work."

DeLucca stepped close, his leather shoe pressed into Kartar's instep. DeLucca's nose, inches away, and the smell of his cologne were suddenly Kartar's entire world. "Are you telling me there's going to be a problem because you didn't manage your team right?"

Kartar gulped. "I'm saying, six months to do re–design, development, and testing isn't a lot of time."

DeLucca's nostrils widened as he snorted. "You worry too much." He walked over to the latest Gantt covering three walls. "I know we've added more work, but we've added people too. The Gantt looks fine. Besides, we HAVE to have this. Marketing's backing Glenn after he promised them Requirements 2.0 would allow us to pull in double what we thought could ever be possible. Marketing loves it! They want to deliver ads based on how the user's feeling. Noah can do that using fuzzy hellistics–or–something. Marketing's already dropped a press release to Wall Street and Sales has advertisers lining up. They want to sell uppers—well, the legal ones —to the players when they look tired. They want to run buffet and food offers when they look hungry. Guest Services will use the camera to save walk–outs. The Winner would let the guy get a minor win, say ten dollars on electronic slots or Whack–a–Drink—anything to get their adrenaline going again—and keep them playing until we get their last dollar. That means more casino operations will need visual dashboards to monitor and support the players, and those dashboards mean UIs beyond what your team's doing. We'll make an Operations Vertical. Noah's going to develop the GUI architecture, and your team stays focused on the games vertical, creating games on top of Noah's architecture."

Standing still seemed best for taking in DeLucca's words. Kartar counted heart beats. At fifteen, he decided he wouldn't burst. Clearly Noah had made his move.

DeLucca chuckled and patted Kartar's shoulder. "You look better now. You had me worried for a moment, and it's not good to make your president worry. I want to congratulate you on all your help with the Requirements. Keep up the good work, and keep those design reviews cooking a little longer. Get this baby finished by summer. We're planning a helluva launch!"

As Kartar told Theckla what had happened, he suddenly felt too weak to stand. He leaned against the wall, then bent at the waist, hands on knees to support himself. "You wouldn't believe the glee in his voice while he bragged about the slew of new requirements. We'll never succeed if we don't adhere to the process. My dad liked to say that if you look behind the car before you back out, you'll never run over anything, and if successful, you'll feel like you're wasting time because nothing's ever run over. But you do it anyhow.

"Dad was talking about a process, and if it isn't followed, sooner or later someone gets run over. We do this—"

"We'll be taking some steps backward," Theckla said.

Kartar straightened, the anger he felt giving him a second wind. "Right! My team developed code for everything they wrote designs for. Maybe our development is half finished. Requirements 2.0 puts a swath of changes across our designs and prototypes. Continuous change means continual rework, and we'll never finish development."

Theckla said, "We need to lock the requirements down."

"Yes. We need to stop these changes."

Theckla shook her head. "Kartar, we're screwed. Once directors smell money, they never walk away. They chase it as inmates would a hot babe with jail keys in her cleavage."

Kartar decided to face the devil himself and called a meeting. As soon as Kartar entered the room, Noah held hands out, palms up, as if to proclaim his innocence. "Kartar, I know you have to be as upset as I am. These Requirements 2.0 are completely unacceptable! WDIWT, WDIWT, WDIWT."

Kartar shook his head, knowing Noah hadn't talked like that to the directors. "I'm not interested in fighting. I've given up. The GUI architecture is yours. I hope your team honors their commitments to support our team with it." Kartar stared out the window as he spoke, watching the casino parking garage. No trill of surprise coursed through when an ad–wrapped van waited at the garage gate—Valentines at the Stardust. So this is how it felt to be standing upon gallows.

Noah said, "DeLucca came to me with that lump of crazy they call Requirements 2.0 after the Halloween party. You would have thought they wanted the Winner to have ESP. The bandwidth these changes demand will blow apart the messaging infrastructure Arch has been building and testing for the past two months."

Kartar repeated DeLucca's words, flat and uncaring, because he truly didn't care anymore. "Your guys have

been developing code? We're still in the Design Phase."
Kartar preferred someone else get killed. From here on
out, he'd keep a low profile. No more arguments with
LG, Noah, or anyone. Especially DeLucca. It just wasn't
worth it.

Noah said, "When we make changes to support 2.0,
we'll have to backtrack and change tens–of–thousands of
lines of code! There's no way we'll finish in time."

Kartar nodded. Everyone had broken process. Was it
too much to ask to only document the design? Would the
Requirements have finished any faster? No. The teams
were held back by the analysts, the directors, and the
project managers trying to get the Requirements correct.
Would only documenting have made the Design Phase
any faster? Perhaps but the question doesn't make sense:
The team tested their designs since everything around
them was going so slowly. However, writing code or not,
Requirements 2.0 meant major redesign.

Kartar thought about the Gantt in DeLucca's office.
"But it's too early to give up on the release date, don't
you think?" He grinned. "According to the Gantt,
development is starting next week. We'll simply use
some of that for redesign. According to the Gantt, it could
work."

Noah winced. "So your tone betrays that you believe
that about as much as I do. And I know your guys have
been writing code too."

"Yeah." Kartar finger quoted the words.
"Prototyping."

"Prototypes are thrown away. You know as well as I
that our developers counted on building the product with
that code. How will your team feel about their estimates if
you start tossing code away?"

Kartar nodded. "All this re–work. We'll need to re–
estimate."

"Yeah. So new requirements mean days of fiddling with design documents instead of writing code. Then it will take days, even weeks to review and re–estimate, knowing the whole time the directors have already decided when it will release no matter what our estimates are. Why waste a month to make a report that confirms what we already know: we won't finish this summer."

"Maybe I don't know that," said Kartar. He watched the parking garage. The van was inside and out of sight. Was it the auditor's?

"Stop being contrary. If we tell the Casino it's going to take an additional year, the backers will drop out. Kartar—focus on me for a moment!" Noah patted Kartar's shoulder and turned him from the window. "So what I'm saying is, let's keep going as all software projects do—building as much as we can, focusing on the necessary requirements. We'll keep the good ones. You have to admit, a mood recognition system would be pretty damn cool."

Noah was energized and focused. He talked on without brushing aside the stray hair caught in his mouth. "Eventually even the directors will see we're going to ship late and they'll 'get real' and focus on only what they really need, which means we can focus too. So we'll ship a year late, but the Winner will make this casino great and we'll all get promotions. Or the Winner will fail and we take that knowledge to our next job, because if it's not this project then maybe it's the next one that'll be great."

Kartar stared into the dream blazing in Noah's eyes, the dream of being the best at what he did, not just at this company but in the entire West coast, and knew Noah'd do it at any cost, even at the cost of the Casino.

Noah's face changed as he shook his finger at something unseen. "You know, if we could get in contact with those stakeholders . . . . Otherwise the auditors could screw this up."

Kartar nodded. "Delucca says they're Vegas old money."

"You don't say. Any guess as to who?" At the shake of Kartar's head, Noah added, "If you get any leads, let me know."

Noah reached out as if to shake hands but reached past to grasp Kartar's elbow, and held it in a handshake of brotherhood. "They're not engineers like you and me. We can fix the Gantt to get us to summer. That way we can work in peace until then."

"But the auditors—"

"Don't know shit!"

Kartar opened his mouth to say 'yes,' but no sound came. He held still, stopping everything: his feet, his breath, even blinking. Saying 'no' would get him nowhere and maybe lose an ally. To be given the chance to see Dharma this summer, he'd agree to anything.

Kartar closed his mouth and swallowed hard. "Yes."

Noah nodded. "It's the right thing to do. We can do some great work with them off our backs.

"Kartar, get me the names of those stakeholders and I'll do what I can to set expectations. Call, email, do whatever you can do to get me some names. Do that and we'll come out fine."

Noah left the room. The dream of glory faded, leaving Kartar in a fog of despondency. He squeezed his ring and thought of Dharma going to college and Lisa with her iPhone engineer.

Noah had said something ingenious and true to life: take knowledge gained here to our next job and maybe the next project will be great. But how would he live to see the 'next one' and how would Noah, knowing who funded the project, keep killers off his back? And most importantly, could Noah be trusted?

He turned back to the window, the garage, and the concerns about the ad–wrapped van. A hundred steps to walk from the Casino's backdoor to the garage. Another hundred and fifty steps to the elevator, ride it to the fourth sub–level, and, finally, the Cadillac. Outrunning the van would be easy. Home free—if he made it. The gun, so light in his jacket pocket, seemed inadequate to even pierce a blouse.

The coast looked clear. Time to make a break for home. He turned to leave the conference room, stopping for his notebook on the table. The conference room's speakerphone was on.

"Anyone there?" he said. When no one answered, he repeated himself and maxed the volume, but the line stayed silent.

Someone had to be on the other end because the connection was still open. Earlier, Donny'd had a meeting with the India team. Perhaps in Bangaluru a phone lay off hook, forgotten.

He closed the connection then noticed his finger smelled odd. Could it be Lovers? He stooped over the phone, nose nearly touching the buttons. The scent wasn't couture vanilla . . . something herbal. Something green.

Kartar's face flushed red as he wondered if someone had listened in on Noah and his conversation.

THE IT MECHANIC

The project continued through winter. Analysts documented Requirements 2.0, developers updated their design documents to support 2.0, and everyone trained new staff. Like last time, March came before any significant headway was made in developing software. Kartar had already warned Noah that it was likely the auditors knew about their conversation and that they shouldn't, by any means, screw with the chart. However 'miraculously,' the Gantt showed a finish on the deadline if no mistakes were made, if the Requirements no longer changed, if the designs didn't need changing, and if little to no bugs existed. The Testing Phase was reduced from three months to one, and as last time, Kartar, Noah, and Donny convinced the directors to slip the release so testing could happen during July. They planned to install the hardware and software and receive the shipments of handhelds in August. On September 1st, they'd launch the Winner.

Every day, Kartar took a different route to work and

each night he took a different way home. Sometimes via the interstate, sometimes via back roads, sometimes half and half. Every few weeks he had an encounter with an ad van. Sometimes it was David Copperfield, twice it was Taylor Swift, and once it was The Book of Mormon. He'd floor the caddy's accelerator and outrun it, although he'd always honor the stop lights.

At home, he'd enter the code into his new alarm system and fall asleep on the couch. New chrome BlackBerry charging on the coffee table beside him. On the mornings after encountering the van, he'd visit a detail shop. After paying $300 for a full detail, he, or the guy waxing the car, or the woman power washing the undercarriage, would discover a radio transmitter in a new location. In June, when no one could find transmitters any longer, he stopped going. It was just as well, because though the car was beautiful, the detailing was eating up his budget.

Sis Love made several appearances at work with her leather portfolio and designer clutch, often meeting with any one of the directors. Donny observed how odd it was that she only ever talked to people one at a time, "Like a cross–examination." And just like last time, the proverbial shit hit the fan in June when the Winner still couldn't be made to work in India. DeLucca didn't break any pictures though. This time around, he threw whiteboard markers at Kartar, Noah, and Donny as he told them their heads were on the line if they didn't release in September. "In fact," DeLucca added, "some very important Vegas people'll lose a lot of money. If you three jag–offs value having long lives, you'll get the Winner released. And that's a fact."

Afterwards, Donny caught up to Kartar at the latte stand and asked, "Was he just threatening us?"

Kartar winced and shook his jacket pocket with the

Colt Pinfire in a meaningful way. They drank their lattes at a round coffee counter.

"Donny, I know you have a bigger gun."

"After today, I'm happier keeping it nearby. It's a free country. Get your own."

Kartar shook his head. "My waiting period doesn't end until next month."

Donny took a pull off his Saturn Sludge, a quad–shot with extra cream and sugar. "Well, I'm sure DeLucca's just making talk."

"He's not," Kartar said.

Donny set the coffee down, hands on both sides of the cup, and stared. "You're not going to start again with those insinuations about Wow being mob–funded and hitwomen in ad vans. Of course I see ad vans! We're in Vegas for cryin' out loud! The mayor probably drives one."

He pointed at Donny. "Don't go on any walks alone with Sis Love. She'll put you in the ground."

Donny slapped the table and laughed. "I got your angle! You want her for yourself, you sly dog!" He walked away with his Saturn Sludge, head shaking and laughing.

At six, Theckla handed Kartar a sealed envelope while he worked.

"It's from Mrs. Sis Love, the loveliest of our lovely auditors," Theckla said, rolling her eyes. She waited for him to open it.

Kartar tossed it onto the desk. "I don't have time now." He repeated the same until she left. Inside was a printed note: Our analysis of change requests and interviews conclude that we have concerns to discuss with you.

"Dammit! What about Noah? Most of this is now his idea."

His neck hairs tingled as he imagined Sis Love nearby with her silenced pistol, aiming to put bullet into his head. Exposing himself as little as possible, he peered around the office. Even though it was evening, many were still at their desks, plugging away. So far, no auditor. He texted Noah on whether he'd also received a message from an auditor, and he sat on his desk, watching the hallway and waiting for Noah's response, chair positioned to obstruct the cubicle entrance. Noah didn't reply.

After an hour, he called Noah but it rang into voice mail. He left a message to call him back urgently. It seemed too risky to drive home after Mr. DeLucca's talk and the note, so he went to the casino floor and sat at the bar. The gin and tonics went down smooth. He drank one after another, as if he'd just emerged from the desert.

The chairs beside him stayed empty. There were two groups at the bar: a heavyset couple from the Midwest drinking Bud, and three college boys drinking Red Bull and whiskey. Kartar stuck with Bombay, an English gin that took the name of an Indian state capitol.

The couple both sported Green Bay Packers sweatshirts. While the bartender and husband talked football, his wife spoke loudly into her cell phone to her daughter.

"Even though you study together, this happens sometimes. You're best friends. She'll get over it. It's not like there's anything wrong with getting a B."

He thought of Dharma and his silent home. Although the settlement was that he'd have Dharma the whole summer, they'd been together only a week before he was murdered. Outside that brief period, it'd been nearly two years since he'd made her morning chai, listened to her running water and the hair dryer in the bathroom, and wished her goodnight. In four short days, she'd arrive for the summer. He couldn't let DeLucca, LG, Noah, his team, or anyone else ruin this for him. He just had to get through June alive, then August, and then. . . .

Because Dharma complained about 'non–emergency voice calls,' he sent a text instead, asking what she'd like to do together this summer. Last time, she was satisfied staying home, playing video games and watching movies.

He gulped down the drink in his hand. The bartender poured another. Dharma hadn't responded yet. She had lots of friends that keep her busy. She was a good girl and would get to his message when she had a moment. And where was Noah? He was usually prompt, sometimes painfully so.

Two of the college students crowded near the third who complained, "I can't believe it crashed again!"

Kartar smiled at how the three studied the unresponsive iPhone. Good to see iPhone engineering ain't all roses.

"What's crashed your phone?" said Kartar.

The three students looked up. "Traffic app," said the phone's owner, a boy with acne along his jawline. "Every forty minutes it blows up."

Another punched his arm. "Yeah, you should've driven faster, then your phone wouldn't crash."

Kartar said, "I thought the App Store kept the garbage out?" Couldn't resist the jab.

The kid made a face while the phone rebooted.

"Apple only does a smoke test." This was said by the mechanic who Kartar had passed by every day. He brushed past Kartar and sat down next to him at the bar, sweeping empty glasses aside with a red toolbox, 'Agile' hand–lettered on its side with black marker. The short man huffed and hefted his butt onto the stool. Once atop, a long sigh escaped, as if needed to release stress from a hard day's work. "They only check to see if the app crashes upon startup and maybe they try some features."

He bumped the toolbox down the bar a bit and set elbows on top to rest chin on hands. An awkward pose, as the bar was as high as the zipper on his breast pocket. The bartender's eye narrowed only momentarily before he set out a napkin and pretzel bowel. This was Vegas after all.

"Try Smart Route next time," J shouted to the young men. They stared open–mouthed, obviously enthralled by the yellow striping across his forehead. J continued, misreading their acute attention as interest in his words. "They build automated tests for all features along with unit testing. Since they're near 100% code coverage, you'll have better luck."

J turned to Kartar, apparently finished with his advice, but the kids continued to glance at J as they mumbled amongst themselves.

Kartar said, "I doubt they heard a word."

J's hair, twisted into messy dreads, reached past his shoulders. The starchy coveralls he wore made his motions as stiff as a stick man in a suit of armor. He swung an arm out and pointed at which bottle of Vodka he'd like, a thin arm that seemed barely able to bend the sleeve.

"You sound like their test manager," Kartar said.

"Acha . . . no. They wouldn't be able to do that if they required a test manager. Their coverage is high because the development team builds test automation with TDD among other things. Test automation doesn't require management."

Kartar had heard of TDD but had never met anyone who'd actually wrote a test before writing any code. Silence stretched on and became awkward while Kartar tried to guess how the man had found him. "Then you're a project manager."

J smiled. White teeth peeked out from under the heavy beard hanging like brush over lips. "No, but I do business with them. I mentored their teams in Agile development, from product planning to 'hands on keyboard' activities such as coding and developing automated tests."

"Agile." Kartar squinted at the bottles on the back shelf. "I'm a little fuzzy inside right now, but isn't that where people don't do analysis and just let developers write code? Impossible with my team. They don't know what to do without a lot of documentation, design, and management."

The man trembled like winter blew down his back, then slowly, like he steeled himself, he scooted himself and drink closer to Kartar.

"I love my team—I mean, we even have nicknames—but they get lost in the casino during lunch breaks and always arrive late to meetings. Requirements Reviews, Design Reviews, Code Reviews, all of them."

The man's eyes narrowed and sucked lips into mouth. His head quivered as if containing a scream.

"What's wrong?" Kartar asked.

He shook his head then gulped vodka. "Indigestion. I'm better now." He pulled a brass colored zipper and slid out something flat and green. "Sounds like you're doing traditional Waterfall then."

Green and flexible, it was a plantain leaf, the same thick and strong leaf used in India in place of plastic or Styrofoam plates. He handed it to Kartar. Written upon it, as if by fingertip dipped in car grease, was:

J Sutherland
Agile Coach
Agile Tree Ltd.

"Aren't you a godman?"

"I can't very well put that on the card. None would take me seriously."

Kartar stared at the man's face coated in Indian color

paint. "Sure . . . . She told you to find me here." He referred to Ma.

"Does it matter?"

"And the toolbox?"

"Tools."

"Your business card isn't even a card, and even so, no number or email. How can a client contact you?"

"On a leaf, write a message and toss it out the nearest window."

It was all too absurd. Kartar stood. "I can't take this right now." He turned to leave.

J's eyes opened wide. "You're right! You can't!" He slapped the toolbox and the lid sprung open. Out he lifted sticky notes and a sharpie.

"Sit. This is what you're trying to do, right?" He moved the sharpie violently across the paper.

Requirements
　Specifications
　　　Design
　　　　Development
　　　　　Test
　　　　　　Deployment
　　　　　　　Maintenance

"When a phase completes, you fall into the next."

Kartar slapped his forehead and sat. "You know, I just realized what bugged me about the Casino's Waterfall. We never did business requirements as a separate step from specifications! We've only got the five phase and we're not even worrying about maintenance." He pinched the ring beneath his shirt. "That would straighten out our requirements problems!"

J stared at him, yellow grilled forehead and blue sideburns framing an impassive face. "Adding more steps and more meetings won't make you more productive." He slapped the toolbox again and the lid swung shut. "The assumptions this process is based on are wrong. In fact, inside the 1970s, Winston W. Royce wrote a paper—"

Kartar snapped fingers together. "I know that name! Art of Navigating Waterfall Projects! He's the founder of the process."

"None know for sure who is to blame."

Kartar glared, but J's eyes stayed pointed. Kartar looked away, feeling like he'd missed some important bit of news that everyone else already knew.

"Dr. Royce wrote a paper[2] about the process he'd used for many years for developing aerospace software projects, the process we now call Waterfall. Each stage has a sluice gate, where management determines if the stage is complete, and if so, they open the sluice and let the water fall to the next stage. As stages complete, there's a feeling of progression. Perhaps we're halfway done when halfway down the Waterfall."

Kartar said, "Or even more than halfway. If you do a good job of Design, the Development and Test phases will be shorter because a good design reduces bugs and makes development easier."

J paused, eyes narrow, mouth open, and then whatever seemed to bother him faded because he emptied his drink. Kartar waved for another.

"Acha, regardless, do you agree that a process gives us rules of operation and those rules have quality gates as a rough way to indicate progress?"

---

2 Winston Royce, "Managing the Development of Large Software Systems," Proceedings of IEEE WESCON August 26: 1–9, http://www.cs.umd.edu/class/spring2003/cmsc838p/Process/waterfall.pdf

"Certainly."

"Upon entering, perchance the Design Phase, your team's creating a design based on the completed specifications, do you ever discover specifications that aren't clear, impossible to implement, or need adjustment, eh?"

"Often." Whack–a–Dollar and the idea to support bar giveaways when the original requirement was for a dollar was only just one such example. Last time, they didn't have Whack–a–anything until near the release date, and LG wanted Whack–a–Dollar. So he had added it from the start. Despite this change, it had morphed into the much harder to build 'Whack–a–Drink,' requiring more meetings between Rockstar and LG, and then even more meetings with the directors and the BAs, and then again, between the BAs and developers. In fact, both times he'd lived through this project, Rockstar's designs seemed to explode more than others. What was going on in those meetings with LG?

Kartar shook himself from the memories. "No matter how often we review requirements, when you work on design, you think deeper and discover something's not clear. So we discuss the requirement with our analysts, and update the documents until the development team's clear on the design."

"Your analysts learned from those discussions. This changed their understanding of how the application should operate, eh?"

"Yeah. . . ." Remembering how Rockstar had called, freaked out because his innocent comment had transformed a feature from something that would take a week to complete into five person months.

"Acha. Whenever both parties have a discussion or do work, they acquire new understanding—"

Kartar made a face. "Entirely new specifications are

created, which means new design work and more reviews. I dread my developers being in the same room as the analysts because someone says something, then five new things need to be developed. Then, if we refuse to do the work, the analysts tell the directors and the directors order me to do it anyhow, and with the same deadline!"

The ice in his untouched drink had melted and overflowed the sides. The puddle reached J's note with the Waterfall diagram and ran the ink of the Maintenance Phase.

When J remained silent, Kartar said, "Even if directors and analysts sign off on requirements, they change them whenever dreaming up something new." He wet his finger in the puddle and drew a Snoopy on the table, with a frown.

J patted his shoulder. "Royce said the flaw in the process was that water didn't just fall, but flowed upward too. He expected that the work of the previous phases would be preserved, or at worse, changes would affect only the previous phase. But he observed that re–work rippled everywhere. Nothing was safe!"

"Mr. DeLucca actually expects to finish on schedule, whether they change the whole damn project or not!"

Kartar leaned back, letting his head loll as if passed out, reliving Winner memories, all the more vivid since he'd experienced it twice.

"Hey!" said J. "Wake up!"

DeLucca was forcing him to carry all the risk.

Kartar clenched fingers into fists, crossed his arms, and flexed his entire body, feeling the injustice build. He held onto it, body shaking, arms quivering. Then jolted forward to mash a fist into the puddle.

"This isn't a waterfall, it's a wave pool! Sometimes it flows downstream, and other times, a logjam forces it to flow back the other direction. It's a complete and utter mess!"

J nodded and smiled at the bartender who glanced their way at Kartar's outburst. "Acha, that's why, even though we're halfway or even three–fourths of the way through the Waterfall stages, we only may be 10% finished. It's guesswork as to what's complete until the Testing Phase!"

"I've had projects extend fifty percent because of bugs discovered in Testing. So I agree. But," Kartar straightened up and faced J, "what can I do when LG wants to add new requirements?"

"Why not let her?"

What was J after with this question? Torture? Just like Ma to set upon him the most infuriating person in India.

Kartar leaned forward, angry, nose inches from this fakir. "Adding requirements after the Requirements Phase is completed breaks the process, so we'd never get done by the deadline."

"How do you know?"

"Because no one allows schedule changes. Today's Gantt assumes perfect execution, but I know there'll be days when no code's written because the team'll be holed up in meetings over change requests or held up by a technical problem."

"Gantt charts do hide a lot of problems."

Kartar lurched back, hands raised. J knew about Noah's fix to the Gantt? Was J in cahoots with Lovers?

J said, "You don't feel confident because you've no reason to be confident." He ticked a finger for each point: "You haven't any software that works. Your test team hasn't been able test anything. Sure, your team's learning how to better use technology to build this daily, but the Waterfall Process discourages them from design changes that take advantage of new understanding. Business gets a clearer idea of what they want daily, but the process discourages using new information to build what they really need, and forces everyone to build what they once thought was needed. All you have for your effort is a stack of documents: Specifications, Requirements, Design, and Test Plans, documents that get distanced from reality, day by day, because they still represent past assumptions.

"Kartar, the Casino can't make money with documents. They need software."

Kartar scrutinized J's face. There's no way this guy could be a plant. He talked too much, and no one outside India would walk in public with colors on their face. Kartar slumped. How had Winner gotten out of control, again?

J pointed at Kartar. "All of this means your Mr. DeLucca will be unhappy. Dr. Royce told the world about Waterfall's failure, but none had an alternative, so we keep beating our heads on the same wall, hoping for perfect specifications, perfect requirements, perfect designs, perfect code, and perfect tests.

He shook his head causing a lock to fall across his face. "But nobody has a good understanding at the start. It's not possible for your stakeholders to know what they want until they see a working product. As the Waterfall Process proceeds, changes in later stages are more expensive to implement, so management throttles change by requiring documentation, sign–offs, and meetings.

"This virtually ensures that what's built isn't what they want, because everyone knows the least at the beginning."

Kartar pulled car keys out and stared at them, thinking again about the ad–wrapped van. So tired of this. If they follow tonight, take a slow drive into the desert and get it over with. But Dharma. . . .

J misunderstood and snatched them away. "You've

drunk too much."

Kartar was stunned. J dropped the keys into his breast pocket, zipped it shut, and kept talking.

No reason to listen any longer, because he was a dead man. No matter what the Gantt showed, the project duration only got longer with every conversation anyone had with his team. The Lovers would keep coming for him, coming with their guns, their hot bodies, their cold demeanors. The Cadillac could outrun them in the van, but eventually he'd make a mistake, and they'd gun him down. Being buried with a Gantt may be a PM's ultimate burden, but it'd be an insult with Noah's doctored chart.

J snapped fingers together before Kartar's face. Kartar startled, wondering how long the man had been doing it.

"Although it's my second try and I know more, I'm doing worse somehow!"

"Hello my friend. Do you understand what I'm telling you? It's your process that's flawed. Stop beating your head against the wall and make changes. Your Mr. DeLucca's right. As he gets more information, he should be allowed to act on it. And your team should change design decisions as they better understand the technology."

The old man was right. Something had to be done. Maybe the gods wanted him to learn Agile. Maybe they put this crazed man before him to show the way.

Kartar nodded. "OK, I'll bite." He slid a pile of napkins over to J. "Show me how Agile works."

J took one from the stack and wrote:

Agile Manifesto
* Individuals and interactions over processes and tools
* Working software over comprehensive documentation
* Customer collaboration over contract negotiation

* Responding to change over following a plan

"Shit! I'm so dead." Kartar's head shook. "This isn't a process! There's no procedure. It's philosophy!"

"Acha. Let's start with the first one. What does it mean?"

Kartar rolled his eyes. Ma had outdone herself enlisting someone this crazy and annoying.

"Are you from an alternate universe where everything's opposite? I'm in this mess because we didn't honor the process, and let people like LG turn every conversation against us."

"Kartar, I perceive you're an experienced project manager who's trying to deliver what his company wants, but knows he can not. Well, you're right. You're on the path to project failure, and if you continue with the process that got you here, you'll fail. Did your Waterfall process deliver any of your other projects on time?"

Kartar rocked back and back, then realized he was going to fall. J caught Kartar's knee and uprighted him.

"I'm sorry. You need to hear it straight. This project needs dramatic change to succeed." He waved at the bartender. "Let me order you a drink. We both could use a cappuccino."

Kartar nodded.

"You've been doing Waterfall your entire career and delivering projects that are either late or failures. Am I right?"

"Winner would be my first failure. But most projects slip schedule. That's normal. Padding's added to handle increased costs."

J nodded. "Acha, same story all over the industry. Isn't it insane to do the same activity over and over again, and each time, expect a different outcome? Do you think this time, your team will somehow get the estimates right?"

Kartar almost nodded because his situation was different with Winner. He was developing the same product and knew what would slow it down.

And still failing!

"We have better requirements this time, but LG is still filing CRs. Not only that, but Theckla, my BA, told me LG adds extra requirements so she has room to negotiate change requests." His face screwed into a grimace at thought of the twelve screens.

"Don't you pad your estimates? If it's difficult for the business to change its mind later, why shouldn't they pad requirements?" J pointed at the first item on the napkin. "How is bemoaning imperfect estimates, requirements, specs, or designs a good use of time? To avoid criticism, everyone pads everything to control risk, adding more noise to the system. We've focused on the Waterfall process instead of people and rarely netted good results."

Kartar fidgeted with his phone, thinking. Wow complained that Arch's quality was poor and on how slow they were. Arch complained that Wow didn't give them good requirements and frequently made CRs. The blue line on the Gantt bounced between the teams in a vicious game of pong, same as last time.

"What should I do?"

J grabbed the Waterfall napkin and crushed it.

"Cease doing that! Forget the Gantt chart. Go to your team and business. Forget the Gantt chart. Tell them what's really happening. Get them talking about what minimum set of functionality must be in your first release." He threw the wadded napkin against the back of the bar.

The bartender raised both eyebrows as he served their cappuccinos. Although J took a deep breath, his chest didn't expand the brown coveralls. "Excuse me. I get passionate because, like you, I used to feel it was my fault. I was always apologizing to upper management about my projects. Here, let me."

J sandwiched powdered creamer between two sugar packets, ripped them open in one smooth action, and dumped them atop Kartar's coffee. A mound of raw sugar crystals mixed with grains of white creamer set atop the foam.

Kartar raised a spoon to stir, but J blocked him.

"Don't! You'll ruin the silky foam. Let it absorb as you drink."

"You have stimulants with your stimulants."

Both smiled while J gave his the same treatment. Kartar studied the manifesto. How to develop a product using philosophy?

"I don't see any process here. Without a procedure that can be done over and over again, there won't be repeatability. Like how our coffees are the same. You used the same wicked process and got the same results." Kartar took a sip, holding his breath to keep from inhaling powder or crystals.

"Agile is process agnostic. It's a way of thinking. It's a way of life. The idea is to find a process that supports it. We'll get to that."

J's nose had creamer on it. But among the yellow lined forehead and steel–blue hair running ear to cheek, the white–tipped nose was unremarkable.

J said, "The next item—"

"Working software over comprehensive documentation. You've said multiple times that all I have is a bunch of 'not very good' project documents. I admit that the design documented at the beginning is never a good design after learning more, so design constantly needs updating. Same for requirements. But you need something to go off of, otherwise, nobody knows what they're doing. I don't think you understand how complicated our product is. There's nothing like it! We have hardware requirements. We have server components. Hell, the Directors have just added new requirements for player emotion tracking."

"Yes, you have a cool product and I'm jealous. I wish I was working on it, though I'd insist on transforming it into an Agile project so we could produce a working system within your deadline instead of only unfinished work and documents. If you were a director, which would you rather have?"

"We've three teams working together! A backend, an architecture, and a GUI. A lot needs to be documented so we can cooperate!"

"And a testing team?"

"Of course! They're in India. That's why we need comprehensive documentation, so everyone has the full picture."

J sipped his cappuccino, and this time, nothing stuck to his face. "Yes, that's complicated. Are the teams, except the one in India, inside the same location?"

"Yes."

"Do team members sit beside each other?"

"Rarely. Two were neighbors until one was moved because he's partly allocated to the architecture team. Noah, the architecture PM, had him moved so he's beside the rest of the Arch team."

"That was at your team's expense, but Noah knew what was good for his team, and he acted on it. I bet if you put your team into one location, next to you, team communication will improve and you won't need to write documentation as if each person lived in a separate country."

"But I'm on the project management floor! I can't sit with . . . ."

"Developers?" Head tilted and eyebrows lowered, J looked like an angry robot. "Then make the project management floor the same ground as the development floor. I'm not saying, nor is the Manifesto, that there should be NO documentation. I'm saying, the legacy Waterfall left us with is the habit of relying on documentation too much. Creating and reviewing documents isn't the same as communicating. And you're spending a lot of precious time on meeting over them. You need to find out how to periodically deliver working software and emphasize that activity instead of documentation."

Kartar shook his head. "Could work with maybe five people, but we have three full teams—"

"Four teams."

"But they're in India!"

J stared, unblinking.

"OK, OK, four teams."

Kartar recollected all the phone calls to Kong, mistakenly thinking Kong had finished a simple design document for CC processing when all along, he'd been having meetings with LG. He'd have seen what was happening if Kong worked nearby. That was a good point.

"If we stop meeting to agree on what we are going to do, and we stop documenting our decisions . . . ," Kartar rubbed his palm up a sideburn and then down the back of his neck. "I've no idea what we're going to do."

"Start testing and developing code." J smiled. "No more writing documents for three or four months of a twelve–month project. Immediately create something of business value. We'll cover the rest of the manifesto later."

J grabbed a blank napkin. "I'm going to describe a process that supports all four parts of the manifesto.

Waterfall encourages the formation of teams who satisfy one function: a team of analysts who analyze and document, a team of developers who develop and don't test every line of code, a team of testers who execute tests and write bug reports, system engineers who only analyze and configure, architects who only design, and so on. In 1986, two Japanese guys, Takeuchi and Nonaka, wrote about a new software development process that uses teams of seven to ten people who have the combined expertise of the individual Waterfall teams. They likened this cross–functional group to a rugby team, because in rugby, anyone can carry or pass the ball to any other, and at any moment, the team may reorganize their positions to score. The software process is called Scrum."

"Scrum?"

"Acha. A word borrowed from a rugby formation where the players form a circle shoulder to shoulder, the ball is tossed into the middle, then the scrum sorts out how to move the ball downfield.

"This is the Scrum Process."

While J drew a diagram, Kartar noticed it was after ten PM and the bar occupants had changed. Their ages now ranged from thirty to an older guy in a faded sweater who sipped whisky from beneath his oxygen mask. Maybe being murdered before reaching forty wasn't such a bad way to go.

J still had vibrant black hair and few wrinkles around his eyes. Seemed ageless in a way, neither old nor young. Could he be fifty?

Kartar looked at the process J had sketched out for him.

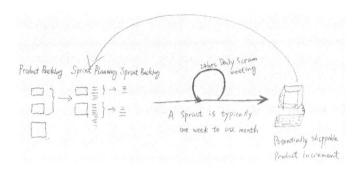

The bottom line was the shortest path to the end and led to something called 'potentially shippable product increment.' 'Shippable' resonated, but 'potentially' sounded weasel–y. But even then it wasn't the end, because a loop brought the line back to the start!

"I'm already worried," he said with a head shake. "It's an unending cycle. And the middle has a second cycle, a meeting every twenty–four hours. Are you saying Agile has MORE meetings?"

"Remember the scrum formation from rugby? A Scrum development team meets daily for 15 minutes. They stand during this time and make decisions on how to move the project forward. It's the most important team meeting. And you're right about the cycle. Scrum doesn't have the satisfying linear, falling direction of Waterfall, but we both know how predictable that process is."

Kartar gave him a hurt look. Guilt over past projects flooded his face with heat.

J continued, Carhartt collar poking his chin. "It's OK. Remember, it's not our fault. Waterfall was inherited, not chosen by you.

"We want as few meetings as possible to avoid interfering with productivity," J continued. "We've found it valuable to have Daily Scrum meetings where the team stops working to check if everyone's effectively moving toward the goal. The meeting is fifteen minutes and everyone stands during it. Seems to keep priorities in order."

"What's this 'Product Backlog?' Is that a requirements or design document?"

"A Product Backlog is a prioritized list of features. At the top are those most valuable to the business. Newly formed Agile teams who already have specifications or requirements can convert them into a Product Backlog. Unlike specifications or requirements documents, backlog items are simple enough to be expressed on a 3X5 note card. Notice what's happening during Sprint Planning?"

Kartar studied the diagram: a subset of the Product Backlog was broken into smaller items.

"Sprint Planning's where the people doing the architecture, analysis, design, testing, and development meet with the Product Owner, the person who manages the Product Backlog."

"Product Owner is what Agile calls the Project Manager?"

"The Product Owner shouldn't a PM as they usually aren't part of the business. Maybe a director. Or maybe a strong business analyst. It needs to be an individual who can attend Sprint Planning with the team, decide the priority of the items on the Sprint Backlog, and understand the business use of the items well enough to discuss and clarify details with the team. It must be one person because, remember, the team's going to start developing software after the meeting. There isn't time for committees to study the problem or to have more meetings to clarify backlog items."

Despite what J said, Kartar decided that living this project twice certainly qualified him to be Product Owner. Or maybe LG? She certainly acted like she knew everything. Mr. DeLucca would be a great Product Owner, but putting DeLucca—Italian shoes, silk suits, the 'old Vegas' attitude—in the same room as Kong, Prince, and Rockstar was a terrible idea. Prince was surly and emotional. Rockstar sometimes had seizures he called 'extreme air–guitar jamming.' Kong was the most normal of the bunch, but that wasn't saying much. DeLucca'd eat 'em alive.

Kartar nodded for J to continue.

"The result of Sprint Planning is a backlog of items the team can finish during the Sprint. As shown here, items may be divided into smaller work items to fit the Sprint's duration. During the meeting, the Product Owner and team may remove unnecessary work or add newly discovered necessary work. Because everyone essential to building the project is together in one room, the meeting's very dynamic. The Product Owner enters carrying a proposed Sprint Backlog and the meeting ends with a Sprint Backlog the team believes is doable within the Sprint.

"The team estimates each item and the Product Owner explains what he wants so everyone understands well enough to make estimates. The work on the Sprint Backlog is limited by how much the team thinks they can finish."

"What's this? A worker revolt? Those guys couldn't estimate their way out of a paper bag. I and the other PMs have taken to doing the high level estimates."

J's head swiveled to face Kartar, steel–blue sideburns pressed against his collar. "When you ship, drop me an email about how accurate those estimates were."

"You think senior people can't estimate well?"

"Assuming you come up with perfect estimates for yourself, you're estimating for your solution and ability. Even if you pad estimates with extra time, others may not be able to develop using the approach you, the estimator, imagined. Better that the people doing the work make the estimates. If you are to do the work, then perfect. But there are better ways to plan a project than treating estimates as exactimates."

"Exact estimates." Kartar laughed. "We understand they're estimates. We pad them so we've margin for error."

"Acha. After padding they become exactimates? How much padding do you add? Industry standard is 30%."

Kartar nodded.

J finished his cappuccino. "Then you're adding a constant ratio to whatever your estimate is. You're assuming you're exactly one–third off, all the time."

Kartar thought about the chapter on Estimation Practices in The Art of Navigating Waterfall Projects. "No. We're 90% confident it'll be no more than one–third under or over the estimation."

"You're saying that adding padding to a large number of estimates will transform them into exactiments. In 2004, a Standish Group poll showed only 29% of software projects were considered a success[3] where 'success' meant all required features and on time."

The yellow grill across J's forehead bent downward. "Why does every PM in the world complain that developers can't estimate, ah? Let's return to Waterfall's failed assumptions."

Kartar made a face when he realized he was now drinking cold cappuccino. "You have a point. We assume every previous Waterfall phase is accurate work."

J nodded. "The error grows in each phase until near the end, when the testing team's left holding the bag in an impossible situation: test a year's worth of work in far

---

3   In 1994 it was only 16%. The CHAOS Report (1994), The Standish Group International, Inc.

less time than planned, and please don't find too many bugs because there isn't much time to fix them. Even with padding, the time to finish is unpredictable."

His phone showed eleven o'clock. Kartar scratched his sideburns, feeling tired despite the cappuccino. There was a problem. "The team decides their own estimates and how much can be done. But what if the Product Owner doesn't agree with them? Negotiating between the team and the business is project management's role. In Agile, where does project management fit in?"

"You don't mean 'in Agile,' you mean 'in Scrum.' Agile is anything that supports the Manifesto. You want process details so let's focus on Scrum, otherwise we'll be up all night talking about other Agile processes[4]. Scrum has three primary roles. Think of them as the three poles of power in a project."

Kartar handed J another napkin.

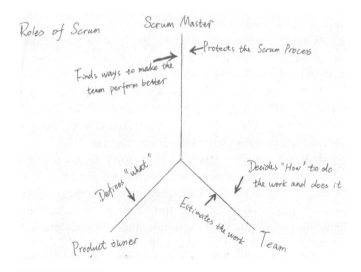

---

4   eXtreme Programming, Kanban, Lean, and Feature
    Driven Development are other examples.

"The team decides 'how' to meet the project goals, the ScrumMaster helps the team be productive using the Scrum Framework and solves the team's impediments, and the Product Owner determines the 'what' needs to be done to meet the project goals."

Kartar shook his head. De'Arte had thirty developers, sixty testers, two BAs, and four project managers. "This process boils down to three roles? What about the BAs, the Directors, and the architects? What about usability engineers? This ScrumMaster sounds like a PM, but what are these imped–mints?"

"Imped–mints . . . ," J's head rotated to Kartar like a robot. "Sounds like something you eat, eh?" He smiled and it was warm, not at all like a robot.

Kartar smiled in return, but only a little.

J tilted his head cockeyed and leaned close, smelling of cardamon. "An impediment is anything that slows—"

Kartar shook his head. "This, this, theory talk is impossible to implement at the Casino."

J's right eyebrow raised. "Theory talk? Scrum came out of industry. The manifesto's original signatories were working software developers."

"Sorry. I'm tired and this sounds impossible: three roles, no analysis, just write code and somehow you get software that works in five to twenty workdays?" Kartar waved fingers through the air. "It sounds crazy!"

"I didn't say NO analysis. Just don't spend months where the only result is another document! Do enough to develop a Product Backlog and prioritize it. Take a portion of the backlog to a four–hour Sprint Planning meeting, and do more analysis to estimate what work can be accomplished during the Sprint. Then after the Sprint starts, more analysis happens as needed while designing, developing, and testing rigorously. At the end, demo a working product to the stakeholders. Then hold a one–

hour meeting to retrospect on how the Sprint went and how to make it more successful. Start the process over again with your next Sprint Planning meeting."

Kartar imagined all the hours of meetings and documentation he'd dealt with somehow boiled down to a four–hour meeting, then his team building something that could be tested and shown to the directors, all within a month.

The team can't even keep the documents up to date. And testing each Sprint—We're a month away from getting an environment up and running in India. How could this . . . mechanic be serious?

"This process will give you what you want, and Mr. DeLucca what he wants."

"No, no, I'm sorry. This may have worked for Smart Roads—"

"Kartar, let's illustrate the process with a simulation." His head shook so quick braids swung into the air. "No, even better. Let's work together on a project. When must you return home?"

J swept back his braids so they hung down his neck, and with a lifted chin, awaited his answer.

"I don't catch your meaning. You mean do a project . . . now?"

"Yes. I'll find one."

J left the bar and moved through the room before Kartar could nod. The area vacated by the college kids was now occupied by two businessmen in suits. They stopped their conversation as soon as the man in brown coveralls stepped up to their table. One watched in disbelief while his companion, entranced by J's painted face, engaged in conversation. J stopped nodding to what the man was saying, shook his head and moved on with a "No thank you" tossed over his shoulder. The man with the oxygen mask watched J approach, a hopeful expression on his face. J acknowledged him with hands pressed together in prayer, bowing his head until his 'center eye' touched his hands. Then J reached for the man's ear, pulling out a carnation—an origami flower made from a yellow sticky note. The man accepted the flower with a beatific smile. J moved on to a woman sitting alone, sipping a soft drink so pensively she wasn't noticing her glass was only ice. Kartar realized he recognized her. She was the owner of the SciFi coffee stand.

While the two talked, Kartar's phone buzzed with a text from Dharma:

'Dad, summer break is almost here! Bought my flight to see you! Miss you so much! Mom's right. Don't like the long sideburns, but love you even if you look like Elvis. See you next week!'

Warmth unfurled from the center of his heart to every corner of his body. Thank the gods for such a wonderful girl!

"Kartar? You OK? Something in your eye?" J's braids hung forward as he stood on the bar's foot rail to look down at him.

"Yes." Kartar wiped a napkin across tearful eyes.

"If you don't feel well—"

"I'm fine." Beyond the yellow grill across the man's forehead and past inky eyebrows were dark eyes filled with intelligence. "J, I want my project to turn out OK. No—I need it to turn out amazing."

"You have my card?"

Kartar slide the leaf out of his jacket pocket, past the Colt Pinfire, and held it up.

"Call me tomorrow and we'll evaluate what an Agile Transformation can do for you. For now, we've another project to focus on. I found a Product Owner who's going to hire us for three thirty–minute Sprints. Normally, I'd discuss Sprint duration with the team, but as your coach, I took pedagogical privilege and made some decisions."

He spoke quickly, toolbox hanging from right hand, the left stiffly gesticulating like the tin woodman in Wizard of Oz. J's white teeth kept smiling through his dark beard. It was all so overwhelming.

"Come!" J grabbed Kartar's elbow. "Let's meet our Product Owner."

SPRINTING WITH A BOLLYWOOD
AUTOBOT

"It's designed to tantalize the taste buds while stimulating body and mind. Plus, the hemp milk adds that Las Vegas 'naughty,' and is actually safer for your health as there's no chance of growth hormones or other dairy industry byproducts," said Debbie.

Kartar sat beside J, the two scribbling notes on stickies from J's toolbox as she talked. Although a frequent customer of SciFi Coffee, this was the first time he'd actually met Debbie. She was in her fifties he guessed, with hair curling beneath a brown cowboy hat that matched the long coat hung on a nearby chair. Kartar ticked off a finger for each ingredient. "You've got Chinese matchta, South American yerba mate, and a shot of espresso—Italy. What are you calling this thing?"

"Next week Casino De'Arte is hosting a science fiction convention and I want attendees to know of this product. It's our homage to Joss Whedon and his visionary movie and T.V. series, Firefly. Think of Firefly as the drink of a thousand years in the future, by which point human kind has blended its cultures together. Do you understand that I need more than posters? I want a way to track user engagement with our marketing."

J asked, "Are you going to run a coupon?"

"Yes. Free Fireflies through the first two weeks, and then two weeks of 'Buy one, get one free.' "

Kartar shook his head. "We're moving pretty fast here. Website?"

"Not yet. Something I've been wanting to get going for some time, but you know . . . I've got a business to operate. I have twelve other stands."

Kartar said, "How can we do this? There's not even a website. It'll take weeks to plan out a site, and the poster, we'll need an artist . . . ."

J's arms stiffly moved sleeves outward. "Hold on! We still need to learn the business goals. There's a format called user stories which contains three important bits of information." Somehow a Sharpie appeared in one hand and a pad of stickies in the other. With the Sharpie clenched tightly in his fist, point downward, he wrote the following as if a mechanical plotter:

As a <user>
I've <something>
That <business value>

"Debbie has done the natural thing of telling us the 'somethings' and Kartar, the implementation in your head may be too complex for the current Sprint. Once we have the rest of the information, we can determine a solution that fits the time remaining."

Kartar put hands out like he was weighing two sets of documents. "This mixes business requirements with functional requirements. Those should be in two separate phases. Slopping them together—"

"Will put all the important information on one sticky. We've used fifteen minutes of our first thirty minute Sprint for planning. Follow my lead and try this out."

Elbow bent at ninety degrees, marker clenched in fist, J wrote the following while asking Debbie questions:

As a business owner
I've Engagement Tracking
That measures marketing effectiveness.

Kartar said, "How you can you do that without a CRM system? Like Salesforce?"

"Debbie, you want to know if people are seeing the poster, right? If we put at the bottom, 'SMS or email some such, and receive a free drink coupon,' would that work?"

Debbie held up a scratched and worn Nokia. "Sure, though I don't know how to make email work on this thing. SMS is better. The barista can reply back."

Kartar sat up at this. "Yeah. And you'll have their phone number in the call log. You'll need to collect the call log at the end of each day."

"Not bad. I'll add that to our closing procedures for our baristas."

"Great!" said J. "Now regarding our user story about the poster—"

"Hey, hold on a minute! Shouldn't we capture Debbie's agreement and get her sign–off? Don't we need to document our decisions?"

"Kartar, in Agile, plans are lightweight because we'll work on them immediately or in the very near future. Each user story is just enough to start the conversation and be a reminder that we'll need future conversations. What we've written is sufficient. We've five minutes left to start our first user story. Let's start with this one and draft the layout on the napkin."

#

Kartar rushed through the Casino to get to the print shop. He slipped between octogenarians moving between slots, and dodged pretty hostesses in short skirts and tube tops. Their third and final Sprint, and he literally ran to get a print of the final product, which Debbie would use to reproduce hundreds more.

J stayed in the bar where the wifi was good, transmitting the work to a shop a block from the casino. Getting the product returned by Sprint–end to show Debbie for approval was going to be tight.

"Kartar—," J's voice came the Bluetooth earwig in his ear.

"What?"

J repeated his words and this time Kartar made out, "Upload is halfway." The voice transmission kept breaking up. Likely due to J's phone also transmitting the Photoshop file. At the printers, paper type needed to be decided on and he'd handle any re–layout issues.

Like a youth at a playground, he visualized everything in his periphery and wove past an excited couple catching coins from a machine, slipped between two teens sneaking away from parents, and brushed passed a group of Asian women with fingers in Vs, posing for pictures. He'd never ran through the casino before, even when late. Why, he asked himself, why push so hard? When had it become more than just a coffee–stand poster? With each Sprint and each user story, they collaborated in design, management, requirement, and quality. Everything about the project was worked on and decided together. Everything he said was listened to, and every idea he brought up was considered. This project, written on three napkins was, at this moment, more important than the Winner. With Firefly, he completely understood every detail, and was involved with every compromise they'd made. With Winner, anyone from BAs, the business, PMs, or developers had changed plans, updated documents, and made decisions in splinter groups. No single person fully understood the product, and many just did as they were told. Could this 'Agile' really work? Could Scrum be used on Winner, a much more complicated project?

He sprinted past flashing slots and slipped by a tour of loudly–talking Chinese. A service cart glided into his path. He couldn't stop, bounced into it, and fell. A bellhop in a marching–band uniform was sprawled over the cart, but had successfully managed to keep all the silver covers atop the food with his own body. Kartar took the hand of a passerby to get up. The bellboy levered himself off the cart. The platters looked undamaged.

Vanilla. Kartar looked over to the strong grip that had helped him up. Sis Love in grey pencil skirt, white silk blouse, and matching grey long–coat. Her clutch was in her other hand.

"Kartar, how lucky to have found you! Could I have a moment?"

J's voice shot through his earwig, "At the printers?"

"Sorry," Kartar said to the bellhop and Sis. He gripped his coat pocket to feel the Colt inside. "Gotta sprint!" He ran for the exit.

Sis shouted from behind, "It's important we speak Mr. Patel!"

Through the door, pass the valet stand, and onto the Strip he went. The monorail glided overhead. Cars jammed the street. People passed by. The printer's shop was down the side of the casino and past the parking garage. A Hispanic man handed Kartar an entertainment card; pictured was a pretty girl blowing a kiss.

"Kartar!" Sis shouted. "I need to talk to you before you leave!" She had followed him outside, standing at the entrance and looking put off.

"I'll be right back," he shouted, dropped the card, and ran alongside the casino's white walls. Overhead was a three–story Mona Lisa. He pressed on, running beneath The Last Supper, and finally came Starry Night, which stretched the rest of the way to the parking garage.

J said, "Are you alive? You don't sound good."

"—alfway there." He stopped to catch his breath.

"I hope so. We've only twenty minutes left. I took the liberty of telling them we have a high priority job and asked they please handle you first. I promised his staff a round of Fireflies for the favor. So you can jump the queue to the front."

Passed the garage ingress, he entered an alley and ran down the gravel road. The seven–story parking garage was on the right. On the left was the back wall of another casino.

J's thoughtful gesture invigorated his tired legs. Amazing how help came from someone in the bar. While a De'Arte PM would've delegated the task to the runner and gone back to checking email, J was continually thinking of ways to make the Sprint more successful.

He threw open the door and entered the print shop like he fled a tsunami, startling everyone. The clerk behind the counter nodded to him knowingly and waved him to the front of the line.

"I've got the file up on the computer now. Take a look at the starship image. It was a little pixelly so I smoothed it a bit, which made it a tiny bit fuzzy."

Kartar's sides ached. He jabbed fingers into them, unable to speak, so he just nodded.

The clerk gestured at the screen which reflected off his

round, Harry–Potter style glasses. "It works out because the product shot is sharp in the foreground, and offset in the right lower corner."

It looked quite good. "Print it!" Out of the printers with ten minutes left, he ran with poster tube in hand.

"Kartar, Debbie and I are moving to the Casino entrance to meet you halfway."

Kartar stopped at the alley that bordered the parking garage and led to the casino. Sweat coated cheeks and dripped from nose. "No! Meet me at the back door—Debbie'll know. The one closest to the garage."

The words came out as a wash of light engulfed him. He turned to squint into headlights. Blinded, he backed off the sidewalk and into the alley. Maybe it wasn't Lovers. Could be someone taking a shortcut. He kept backing. Standing still would make an easy target. He waved the poster tube as if it was a pipe, hoping it'd distract them. Each step backward he cursed Donny for giving him the tiny Colt. How could his fellow PM keep the good gun for himself? Why hadn't he purchased a proper gun? He'd let work consume him. That's why Lisa divorced him. He always got consumed.

The engine roared and the vehicle accelerated towards him.

"Shit! I knew it, I knew it, I knew it," he said, turning and running as fast as his exhausted legs would move.

J spoke, "Kartar? Kartar? What's happening?"

Down the alley he sprinted. Against the walls on each side, shadows of himself mirrored his struggle. Arms pumping, legs pushing, silhouettes of him stretching ahead as the van closed in, the poster reaching to infinity from a spectral hand. He tossed it over his shoulder. The engine's roar that filled ears was punctuated with the beat of Irish step music. Headlights heated his back, and pebbles pinched by tires ricocheted off alley walls like little bullets. Grasshoppers jumped from and into the violence, their bodies ticking loudly against the grill and headlights just inches behind. A moth barreled into his eye, blinding him. He dove to the side. The van skidded, tires slipping inches past his feet. The door on the passenger side opened. Kartar turned and ran in the other direction, away from the casino.

Taillights diminished as backup–lights flared on. Kartar sprinted past dumpsters as the van pursued in reverse, transmission whining.

"Kartar? What is happening?" J's voice in his ear. His earwig was still connected.

"No you don't!" Kartar shouted, realizing the plan had become 'hit–and–run' instead of blatant homicide. "I won't make it easy!"

Closing on the alley mouth, he readied himself to go right, run up the block, and circle back to the casino. Up ahead, taxis, convertibles, and limos passed in both directions over four lanes. The lights of a monorail station glowed from across the street and further down the alley.

It's not going to work, he realized: Go right, the van would follow traffic and catch up within half a block. Go left, they'd just run him down on the sidewalk.

Mad with fear, Kartar sprinted into the street, looking neither left nor right, springing into the hands of the gods as he decided what must be done to survive: the monorail! Ride it straight to the airport and get the hell out of Vegas.

Tires squealed and a black limo skidded past, 'Good Times 4 Girls' written in pink lettering on the door. Kartar couldn't stop. Her window down, a woman with a 'Bride to Be' tiara watched in shock as Kartar tried to avoid the car, lash extensions and heavy makeup accentuating the wideness of her eyes. A hand brought to open red lips covered them in horror as Kartar slammed into her door. He spun against the limo as it continued skidding past. More headlights lit him from either side. Staggering into the next lane, he willed the spinning world to stop its maddening rotation. He found the station lights of the monorail and focused. Got to the center. Two more lanes left. He leapt off the traffic island and ran for it. Headlights dipped as cars braked. Tires squealed. Horns blared. Safe on the other side, he glanced back to see what the van would do, assuming they'd drive around the block, giving him time, but no! The van took advantage of the turmoil. The traffic had entirely stopped in Kartar's wake, so the van simply followed his path across all four lanes.

"No!" he shouted and ran for the station. Van headlights rebounded as the vehicle bounced over the center island. The moving steps of the escalator were just feet ahead when the van roared from behind, sounding so loud and fast he was certain he was pavement pizza. Tourists gawked from the escalator as he closed in. Something caught his foot—the bumper. He tumbled, crashing into the foot of the escalator. The van slid to a stop and backed away.

"What in two shits Hell?" said a man with a cowboy hat. He stared at the van and gave Kartar a hand up. "Am I hearing Riverdance?"

"Vegas is weird," Kartar said. Bruised and exhausted, he staggered onto moving steps and let the machinery whisk him to safety. Blood dropped from nose onto stair ridges, and more seeped through one trouser knee. Earwig hung cockeyed but no phone—must've gone astray in the chase. Having people nearby felt like safety because they wouldn't kill him in public. Glances slid over him, like he was drunk or homeless. After buying a pass and water from a vending machine, he cleaned the blood off his face and waited for the train. As soon as it arrived, he boarded and sat opposite of the door to watch the platform. Striding off the escalator, gray long–coat billowing in the wind like wings on an angel of death, was Sis, hair now beyond shoulder length and red.

Her eyes widened seeing Kartar through the open door. Kartar froze, willing the doors shut. She sprinted across the platform, vaulted over the payment barrier, and rushed for his car.

"No!" Kartar fumbled the Colt Pinfire out of his pocket. J's leaf fell onto the floor. "Close! Close!" The train sounded warnings that the doors would shut. A little boy picked up J's leaf and held it up, his mom sitting alongside him on the train's bench seat.

Kartar ignored the boy and held the gun tightly at his side, hidden. Shooting a woman seemed wrong. Sis closed the distance between and seemed to have no gun. But the desert, the gantt chart, the way she coldly shot him. She had given no quarter.

So neither would he.

The boy poked him with the leaf while he aimed. Sis dodged as he fired. The gun barely shivered, its report nearly unnoticeable beneath the door closing warnings. The smell of gun smoke filled the car. He fired again. Sis leaped for the next car's entrance just as the doors slid shut. She landed in a roll and finished in a crouch behind a bench, watching.

He fired again and a spot of blood appeared above her breast, now uncovered by the coat.

Fury spread over her face. "I'm insulted you actually hit me with that."

Passengers took that as a cue that something was seriously wrong. The mother covered her son and screamed. Her husband yelled. Everyone watched Kartar.

"No! It's her! She's trying to kill me!" Kartar shouted as the train started to move.

"Is that a gun?" bellowed a well–dressed man.

"Is it real?" said the young boy, peering over his mother's arms.

"Yes!" said Kartar. He snatched the leaf from the boy's hand and fired again at Sis. The shot clipped a handrail. Everyone stayed seated. Some lifted purses for cover, others used magazines or shopping bags. The gun clicked empty on the next shot.

"Damn Donny and this stupid little gun."

Sis straightened from her squat. Kartar flung the pistol and struck her cheek.

"You!" she shouted and stepped forward, cautiously but determined.

Have to get out, he decided. Vertical pole and leaf gripped in one hand, he hit the emergency stop with the other. Sis stumbled and fell. He pulled the door open and exited.

Alongside the elevated monorail was a catwalk. The sound of alarmed passengers faded as he ran on gridded steel above Vegas. Excalibur, the shiny plastic exterior glowing like a toy castle. Luxor's black pyramid piercing upwards, a thorn to keep the gods' hands off of Vegas. New York–New York, a tall and thin Cartoon Network version of downtown Manhattan. The monorail and catwalk stretched onward above a river of traffic lights two stories below. Until the next stop, there was no way to disappear into Vegas fantasy land. So he kept running. Sis exited the car, dropped to a knee and aimed.

Kartar never heard the shot. He jolted. No breath. He teetered at the edge, leaning far over the safety rail and the plummet to the street, recovered, and backed up to fall the other way, onto the train's rail. Something warm filled his mouth. He coughed blood. Something was wrong. He couldn't get up as she advanced.

"You didn't finish on time. You were warned and

warned Kartar, and now you're just an embarrassment."

Kartar cried out, "Don't do this! I've a daughter! She's coming to see me." Feeling returned to arms and legs. He pulled himself along the cement rail, gaining inches further from her.

"Forget family matters. This is business, not personal."

"You're a priestess of the PMI. You must understand how this business goes." Kartar shouted, back arching in effort, hands thrust forward like they could block what was coming. "You know! You have to know projects go late!"

She stretched her stride to set one foot on the monorail, straddling the gap. Her foot blocked him from sliding away. Her coat flared open in the breeze, uncloaking her to the headlights of the Strip that ran below in a river of light, white silk shirt gleaming, red hair matching spots of blood from her wound. The unblinking eye of a pistol with silencer staring down at him.

"But . . . but . . . I've got another way." Kartar held the leaf to her. "I can change things to make it better! We're going to build more software and less documents. We're going to show something working every month. And we'll test as we develop."

Sis leaned close to read the leaf. Scent of vanilla. Red hair brushed his cheek.

"That's rich! Noah's finished the architecture. Donny's built the database. But you've had twelve months and delivered nothing of value."

Before she could straighten, Kartar caught the hair and jerked downward toward the gap she straddled. She jerked upright in response, still in her lunge, feet wobbling and arms thrown out for balance. The wig came free and fell to the street below.

"Jerk!" Recovered, she aimed the gun. "I'll need to get that."

And then nothing.

Kartar lay dead, corpse lying crosswise the monorail track. Blood oozed from the hole in his forehead. Just beyond fingers, the green leaf, his face turned to it like he read its words in death.

SCRUMMING IN A WATERFALL

Instead of being dead he woke up in bed. The project started—Again. This time he'd swim with the Waterfall but prepare his team for change. Let the rest Waterfall, he decided. Wow'd do Scrum.

So he started with his team's requirements and that meant meeting with Thekla. . . .

She tapped her glasses against the conference room table for a moment. "Why this prioritization by business value? I have all the requirements documented right here."

"Because they're going to change," Kartar said. "I want the team to start on the most valuable features. You see, what's 'most valuable' is less likely to change than the 'least valuable.' And even so, it's OK because we'll adapt as we go, using the latest knowledge. An Agile principle is to 'harness change for the customer's competitive advantage.' "

Theckla squinted at him then at the Scrum process diagram on the whiteboard. She slipped her glasses back on. "I see. Adapt."

"You think I'm out of my friggin' mind, don't you?"

"Well, friggin' isn't quite strong enough, but close."

Kartar smiled. His mobile played a tune, signaling a text from Dharma. After a glance he focused on Theckla. "When was the last time a project passed Requirements Complete and never needed a bunch of additional CRs?"

Theckla's eyes narrowed. "Well . . . something like, never? We always miss something. But it's not all the business's fault. Sometimes development or operations asks for something they didn't think of earlier."

"Exactly! So let's accept this fact and use a process that accommodates change. To do otherwise would be bad planning, right?"

"We have a change request process."

"Except it doesn't work very well. Each CR requires lots of meetings, checkpoints, and documentation."

"Kartar . . . . We don't want changing requirements to be easy or people will change them all the time."

"Why shouldn't the business be able to change their mind?" He reflected on how Whack–a–Drink was a great new idea. "And think about changing design specifications too. Development should be able to adapt and design based on new knowledge, new understandings. And Ops should be able to discover missing work items and ask for changes when they pop up."

Theckla lifted hands in a shrug. "But Kartar, it's one thing organizing your team to sit together. But this . . . ." She pointed at the whiteboard. "This is really different! How are you going to get people to do this? Everyone knows how to work with Waterfall's phases. We're used to the meetings and the documents and the sign–offs. How are you going to get Arch and Ka–ching onboard? And . . . how are you going to build reports? Your work–breakdown structures, capacity planning, and the Gantt

. . . ."

He nodded and brushed back his pompadour.

"Yes, I'm aware of all those challenges. I'm just going to change my team. Regarding reporting, I'll handle that. But I need your help. We don't have a Product Owner. Ideally it would be LG or DeLucca, but . . . ."

"Yeah! But you don't want to have this blow up in your face!"

"C'mon, I wouldn't put it that way. Our project's already in a failure mode."

"Huh? How can you say that? We haven't even finished the first phase yet—"

"And we won't know how much trouble we're in until the Test Phase—another problem with Waterfall! For now, I want you to choose one or two requirements my team can start work on while the rest of IT continues with Waterfall. I'll keep my team out of review meetings as much as possible. Maybe only one person will attend—"

"Kartar!"

"Hold on. Because I want them to start developing—"

"Kartar!" Theckla stood, eyebrows arched above glasses and mouth hung open for a good half minute. "You're mad! How can you start DEVELOPMENT before requirements are finished?!"

"And test."

Her mouth clamped shut into a hard tight line, and for a moment, Kartar thought she might actually scream.

This was going to be harder than he'd imagined.

#

Prince, Hong Kong, and Rockstar emerged from the meeting looking dazed. Theckla and Kartar stayed and continued to talk. Rockstar turned to the others and held up a handful of sticky notes. "Can you bloody believe it?

We—us most brilliant developers—start developing today?!"

Prince and Kong perked up, shaken from their stupor. Prince looked down at the sticky notes adorning his chest. "I don't know. I feel kinda dirty. We're skipping straight to the good part without 'paying our dues.' " He giggled like a child.

Kong nodded in agreement. "This is how we did it at the university." He poked Prince's arm. "But it's like how you said. If it feels too easy, then it must be wrong. Professional software engineering is supposed to be lots of meetings and documentation. Right?"

Prince shook his head. "I don't know. I'm not going to complain. He said he'd keep us out of meetings except: Sprint Planning, Retrospective, Sprint Demo, and Daily Scrum."

Rockstar waved at the meeting room where Kartar and Theckla's voices were getting louder. "That is the brilliance of our Indi Elvis. In return, we must actually build this thing and get it working. In TWO weeks! We do that, we'll be the bee's knees!"

Prince raised his hand in a high five. "Yeah! It'll really be a Sprint!" The three slapped hands. "The planning meeting was so intense! We spent more time analyzing what we'll do this Sprint than we ever did in review meetings."

Kong said, "We better start coding. It's strange. Every project I've been on starts with a bunch of slow stuff, but everyone is happy. Then at the end, it's all pressure and trouble. With this Scrum, we get in trouble two weeks from now."

#

Kartar stood in his cubicle with Kong, Prince, and

Rockstar. The Daily Scrum had been going for 30 minutes, and Kong still rambled on about problems integrating with Arch and Ka–ching. His user story had dependencies on architecture features and Donny's team's backend.

Kartar finally couldn't take anymore so he called a timeout. "OK, I get it. You're blocked good."

Kong ticked his tongue. "Every story will have the same problem. It's too early. We can't build the GUI when have nothing to hook too."

"Damn," said Kartar. "Let me think about this and see what I can come up with. Maybe I can pressure the others to start developing too."

The developers looked dubious. Kong said, "They're reviewing requirements. We could do that too so we aren't waiting."

"Hmm—," Kartar said.

Prince snapped fingers together. "We're doing MVC right? Why not have the controller do nothing? And we can build—"

Kartar waved both hands. "OK! I'll take the issue offline. Let's talk about your work Prince. Use the three questions: what you're doing today, what you've accomplished, and impediments."

Prince's face turned red. "Wait! I want to talk about Kong's—"

"Later," Kartar said. "Kong took thirty minutes and we should've been finished in fifteen."

Rockstar nodded vigorously. "Kartar, we all have the same problem. Our status is beastly. We need to integrate our GUI into something!"

"I've an idea!" said Prince.

"OK, so you're all stuck." Kartar made a note. "It's my job to get you unstuck. I'll talk to Donny and Noah."

"But—" said Prince.

"Meeting over!" Kartar checked his phone. "I'm late. I've a requirements review I'm attending in your place." Kartar shooed them away. "Get back to coding, and I'll see what I can do."

Prince's face turned red again. "There's nothing for us to work on if we wait for you."

Kartar waved them off while he rushed to the elevator, a thick requirements document tucked under one arm.

Prince turned to the others. "We've only six days before Sprint end."

Kong patted Prince on the back. "Indi Elvis is the boss. We have to do what he says."

"Take it easy chap. Kartar is managing this project. He got our advice. At the end of the day, the plan is his and so is the project. Odds are, he's under a lot of stress. Let's scrum beside the espresso stand and kotch a bit."

Prince straightened his posture a bit. "Yeah . . . . When you put it that way. We can always transfer to Arch or Ka–ching if Kartar can't make good Sprint Plans."

#

As LG, Theckla, Noah, and Donny began to exit the requirements meeting, Kartar pulled Noah and Donny aside. "I need to discuss something with you." He closed the room again.

Donny sat, forehead wrinkling as eyebrows rose toward sunglasses perched above.

Noah stayed standing. "So . . . can't we do this over email? I have another meeting in fifteen."

"Better sit down," said Donny. "Kartar's got some big secret to share."

Kartar went to the whiteboard and drew their three–

tier architecture.

Noah sat and said to Donny, "Something's happened. Recently, it's only Kartar who comes to our review meetings."

Donny grinned. "Mechanical turks!"

Kartar stopped drawing. "Huh?"

"You're the only one left on Wow because you've replaced your developers with androids."

Noah smiled. "Right! So they aren't androids. They're small men from Turkistan operating each android from inside."

Kartar looked at the two. "Am I the only sane one here?"

Donny winked. "That's rich! Let's go Elvis. Whatcha got for us?"

Kartar wrote on the board 'Simple Slots' and 'Paypal.' "Wow has started developing these two, but of course we have dependencies on the architecture to connect us to the game server."

The clatter of Donny's pen falling to the table turned Kartar's head. Noah leaned his chair back and grinned.

"I have to hand it to you," said Noah, "I've always done a little development during Design, but I've never heard of starting before requirements were completed. Ballsy."

Kartar moved to the right, or tried to: although he felt movement, his feet were stuck. A numbness spread through his limbs, then a tingling. Carefully, he twisted himself back to the whiteboard and focused on drawing the diagram but the dizziness didn't leave.

He turned to his audience. "I don't feel very—" Something had happened to Donny and Noah because neither moved; not even an eye blink. The world had stopped. Time was frozen. The feeling of dislocation would pass; he knew this from before. So he readied himself to repeat what he'd told Theckla; that requirements are never complete, that teams should produce value immediately rather than wait for months to pass. But Donny and Noah ... they weren't going to listen. This change was too big. They'd never accept it.

"We're prototyping." The spell broke. Tingling faded. Donny's head moved, and Noah rocked forward. "I need your help in getting the prototype working."

#

Theckla breezed into Kartar's cubicle. "Thought I was late! You know, with a fifteen–minute meeting, you take more effort to be early, 'cause if you're late, you miss the boat."

Kartar smiled. "The boys are late today. It's ten after."

"An elevator is under maintenance. Maybe that's what's holding them up."

Kong, Prince, and Rockstar exited the elevator and entered Kartar's cubicle, slipping past the small circular table and guest chair that all manager cubicles had. Prince coughed and straightened the collar of his ridiculous polo, the top half leopard print, the bottom, tiger.

Theckla studied him. "Where did you get that?"

Prince smiled. "A fashionista never dresses and tells."

"Sorry we're late," said Kong.

Rockstar smirks. "Kartar, you need to promote us all to PMs so we can be on the same floor."

Kartar nodded. "I really should. Since you've started sitting together, regardless of on–time or late, you arrive together. Much better than our old 'trickle–in' meetings." Everyone nodded. "Rockstar, start with status." Saying it that way felt wrong as soon as words left his mouth. Something in the manifesto about motivation, team, and ownership. Need to review it again.

Prince nodded. "The problem is we're still stuck until dependencies are resolved. To get something done, Kong and I worked on a design document—"

Theckla smiled triumphantly. Kartar shook his head. "The problem is we need to create something valuable before Sprint end—"

The developers and Kartar naturally formed a circle. Theckla stepped deep into the middle. "But guys! Design documents are valuable!"

The developers nodded agreeably.

Kartar shook his head. "Theckla, what do you want the most? As Product Owner."

"A successful project that delivers on time and on budget."

Kartar nodded. "And that project is supposed to deliver what?"

"The Winner—"

"If we deliver design documents every Sprint, will your investors earn money with them?"

"But they help . . . . No. I can't earn money with design documents. I need software."

"So team, what should we be building?"

Prince said, "We can't. We're dependent on the backend and architecture team. We're stuck!"

Kartar handed documents to each person. "This is the agreement I got from them."

They all flipped through the document; Kong made comments out loud. "Interfaces for CC processing, interfaces for Super Simple Slots. This should get us unblocked!"

Rockstar waved the document until it fluttered like a flag. "Wait! Our Sprint ends in a few days. They're going to implement all this before then?"

Kartar cocked his head to the side and glanced downward. "Well . . . no. They won't start until much later."

Theckla said, "How will we get working software?"

Prince shook his head and crumpled the document in his fist. "This is what I tried to tell you earlier. WE could implement the models we need. And our controller could use objects that stub the interfaces. Then those interfaces become the specs for Arch."

Rockstar stood on his toes and paged through the document, rocked back, then onto his toes again. Everyone paused because that was how Rockstar thought —kinetically. After a few more back–and–forths, he spoke up. "This gaming interface here is going to be a problem. It's missing some parameters." Kartar felt his face twisting into a pained look, at which Rockstar added, "But we can work around that problem."

Prince shook his head. "See? We should have implemented the models and interfaces first, tried them out, then spec–ed them for Arch and Ka–ching."

Kartar swept hand over pompadour, closed eyes, and said, "I was rushed. Noah and Donny want everything spec–ed ahead of time or they were going to give me trouble for immediately starting development." The clock showed they'd been standing for forty minutes. He really needed to sit.

He switched to his confident voice. "Come on guys, this is enough to get started." Only Kong nodded in return, and hesitantly at that. "Great! We'll get our stories finished using these interfaces."

As Prince left with Kong and Rockstar, Prince mimicked slapping himself across the face. "Next time I have a good idea at standup, tell me to stick to status reporting. I wouldn't want to get in the way of management's creativity."

Kong said, "You complain about nothing. Try living in China. That government constantly reminds everyone to stay out of its secrets, because it knows best."

#

The month finished with some successful Sprints, but Kartar was bothered by the problems. On the way to getting a latte, he wondered about J. There's been no sign of the mechanic since Firefly. It'd be nice to have a deeper conversation about Agile. How could he get in contact using a leaf? Ridiculous idea, but coming from a guy colored like an Autobot, he thought it best to give it a try, so he sent a text to Ma, asking her to express mail a box of plantain leaves and thought more on the manifesto.

Theckla had hated it at first, but after a few Sprints, she came around to 'working software' as the primary measure of progress. The team was genuinely happier, not having to constantly meet over documentation, but they lacked confidence that the results would be good. Days spent on documentation engendered faith, ill–placed perhaps, but faith nonetheless.

The barista handed him the usual, a RIP Pluto, when suddenly, Theckla was at Kartar's elbow and guiding him to a quiet corner.

"We need to talk. You can commemorate the loss of our 9th planet later."

"What's more important than reliving a dwarf planet's glory days?" The grin stopped at her bleakness.

"Just got a bunch of new requirements from DeLucca."

"Let me guess. Whack–a–Mole—"

Her eyes widened. "How—How do you do that? Did you bug DeLucca's office? No! Don't answer! If you get fired, I'll be left holding the bag and explaining to the rest of IT why we're doing this Agile thing."

She thrust out her palms out to stop his angry

response. "OK, OK. I admit it's really nice to see the application running on a simulator every Sprint. Surprisingly, I got a lot out of seeing Single Wheel Slot. The next Sprint, they added four wheels using my feedback from Single Wheel Slot. That worked very well."

Kartar froze in place.

Theckla noticed and pouted. "Ok. You're right, it was awesome." Her face brightened. "I normally don't do UAT until a few weeks before rollout. But during our Sprint, I'm able to give the team feedback on something working, which is amazing. But, Kartar, DeLucca stresses me out."

Kartar took a pull on his Pluto. "Me too. He keeps skipping Sprint Demos and insisting I fill out status reports and risk assessments, which take hours out of each day. If they'd only come to Sprint Demos, they'd see everything, ask questions, and get the REAL status. Why not have a face–to–face conversation about the project, instead of burying me in requests for reports they aren't even reading!"

He was loud enough that the barista and Donny's team glanced their way. Kartar closed his mouth for a moment, then started speaking in softer tones.

"I expect I'll eventually get DeLucca's attendance. But LG wants 'sign–offs,' so she has somewhere to lay blame."

Theckla scrunched her nose. The frames of her glasses raised clear above her eyebrows. "Yeah . . . . There are BAs that work for good or for evil. LG's somewhere in the middle."

"You're too kind." Kartar looked around the lobby as developers from Arch exited the elevator and went to the coffee stand.

Theckla said, "Back to Whack–a–Mole. So what

should I do with these new requirements? We could start review meetings. Your team can respond by writing tech specs and design documents—Ok, so either something is wrong with your Pluto or you hate the idea."

Kartar set the drink down and simply stared.

Theckla said, "You're not being reasonable! There's no way we can say no! We're in Requirements Phase—er, supposed to be—so we can't cry foul."

"This new requirement is fine! Let's 'respond to change over following a plan,' and you and I put together user stories for Whack–a–Mole and bring them to the next Sprint Planning." Kartar finished his drink. "Easy peasy." He dusted his palms together.

"But we're not finished with our first game!"

"And," Kartar said, "Don't forget we're still missing a bunch of architecture and backend. So what we have isn't shippable, and won't be, until Noah and Donny enter Development. And don't even get me started on how badly telling Mr. DeLucca that I already wanted a test team went. He just said, 'no,' and asked for more status reports."

Theckla smirked. "When Noah and Donny saw your change requests, they never realized we were actually building it—Now! Oh, the looks on their faces! They couldn't figure out how you got such detail in your document."

Kartar glared as he spoke, "THEY have nothing to complain about. They're in Requirements Phase, and I'm sending them new requirements. They haven't written a line of code. Every feature we create is dependent on them. Do you know that they represent the biggest risk to Wow?"

"Come on! Lighten up! We're all in REQUIREMENTS Phase. Maybe we'll have the entire GUI done before they enter Development."

"Yeah . . . ."

Theckla squinted at him. "If something is wrong—"

"No! I'm just . . . I wish I could get Noah and Donny to build what we need now so we could at least do integration testing."

"Slow down! It's not like we're releasing next month."

"That's the problem! The way we're working, it's not possible to do it." Kartar frowned. "We need to get off the simulator and onto hardware. If Noah and Donny would coordinate with us, we could actually put the Winner, with five wheel slots and PayPal payment processing, into players' hands."

Theckla rolled her eyes. "Yeah! And if I had a magic wand, I'd give a pony to every little girl. You're not being reasonable! You can't ship a one–year project in two months."

Kartar nodded. "You're right. But I'd like to ship one–twelfth or one–sixth of the total project every month or so. When we get new things like Whack–a–Mole, we just release enhancements to what the players are already using."

"Relax Elvis! You'll develop worry lines!"

Kartar nodded. New posters were up regarding a gun show. Tonight he'd file for a concealed weapon permit. Things were fine now, at the beginning, as always. With a little preparation, he wouldn't be the victim this time, no matter what.

#

It was the same game as before. October, four months into the project, DeLucca's stakeholders became nervous, and DeLucca responded by doubling the required status reporting. Each night, Kartar sent reports with Gantt updates and the latest work breakdown. To call the reports 'creative' was understatement. It needed to show the team had things to do for the rest of the year, and so it did.

Because they did iterative development and used a productivity metric called 'velocity' to manage their capacity, he had to invent numbers to show they'd be busy in the upcoming months. Waterfall utilized the 'Perfect Planning Method,' which used estimates for work to be completed in the future. If you estimated to take two hours to mow a lawn, then plan for two hours. With the availability of two people and two mowers, then the job could be done in one hour. Four people and four mowers, then thirty minutes. Of course, every project manager knew there was always overhead to consider, so buffer time was added. A constant buffer, just as J had said. Each night, the report showed a day's worth of progress that had been made against the "unchanging plan," which was Kong, Rockstar, and Prince multiplied by a nine hour day, resulting in twenty–seven dev hours. And nine hours instead of eight, because it looked more impressive to upper management who still believed a well–managed team was an over–worked team. No project manager wanted to tell his boss the project was behind schedule, and no one worked overtime. It just wasn't done.

But with Agile, the team used 'story points,' which was a system for assigning an abstract number to a work item. Abstract in the sense that the number wasn't based on real–world units as in hours or days. These numbers were arrived at using a process called Planning Poker, which his team loved. Hell, they worked in a casino. And who didn't love poker? The abstract numbers came from a nonlinear numbering system, such as the geometric series, eliminating wasteful arguments over whether a user story was one hour or ninety minutes. A trivial difference for a multi–week Sprint.

During Sprint Planning, each team member had playing cards, one card for each number: 0, 1, 2, 4, 8, 16, 32, 64, and 128. Like a casino dealer, Kartar slapped a user story onto the table, and each team member, secretively like in poker, decided what card represented the difficulty of implementing the story. Once ready, they'd reveal what card they'd chosen at the same time.

For the Whack–a–Mole story, when Prince showed sixteen, Kong an eight, and Rockstar a sixty–four, divergence in understanding was quickly revealed. So Kartar asked Kong to tell the team why he believed the story to be an eight and Rockstar why he'd chosen sixty–four. Kartar limited discussion to five minutes to prevent them from planning every detail. They talked about 'right–sized' details: particulars that informed others why they selected that card, and through discussion, corrected the group's understanding until they were all on the same page. Next, Kartar called for playing another hand on the same story, and again, each selected a card, revealing their estimates together, resulting in a much smaller divergence than the previous try. The process worked amazingly well, usually needing no more than two poker hands per story. They regularly estimated a Sprint Backlog within a two–hour meeting and afterwards, started developing.

Since the rest of Casino IT used Waterfall and Perfect Planning, Kartar had to fill out paperwork in a way that DeLucca (or whoever) could understand. If he simply said that, for the last eight Sprints, the team's velocity (the sum of story points finished in a Sprint) had averaged forty story points, he'd have uncomfortable questions from an angry boss who wanted to avoid looking bad. So each night before leaving the office, Kartar took the latest version of the requirements document and mapped to them the day's accomplishments. Those requirements had Perfect Planning estimates in hours he'd made up using a conversion from velocity back to hours: velocity / (hours–in–a–Sprint X three–people).

Even so, it wasn't easy because Waterfall made another assumption: a work breakdown structure (WBS) that assigned a year's worth of work assigned to each individual while assuming they never collaborated with others and that having problems was a rare.

Essentially, Perfect Planning was perfectly wrong. The team not only estimated together, they also collaborated on each story, pairing up to write code (pair programming). All in all, it required hours of extra work to represent his Scrum team as a Waterfall team in a report likely nobody read. The report did nothing to help the project, having little to do with working software. This meant reporting actually hurt the project by taking him from valuable work, he realized. He remembered the time he ran to the print shop for Firefly, and J's valuable deed of calling ahead to assist, rather than busying himself with the usual 'PM work' of updating reports. Since everything was visible to Debbie, she never needed a report.

At nearly 7PM, Kartar was about to hit 'send' on such a report when a text arrived from Dharma:

'Dad, going to a movie tonight with friends. Would be awesome if you saw it too so we could talk about it. Say you'll go tonight!'

Warmth and love coursed through him as he typed back 'YES!' The room began to spin, like being on merry–go–round. He held still, breathed through his mouth, willing the dizziness to pass. Fingers, then hands, itched with invisible ants that marched ever higher, swarming at elbows and then climbing biceps. He gasped like a drowning man while the invisible tramp proceeded up his neck. He looked upward, alarmed to be dying. The ceiling spun lower and lower, advancing downward to crush him. He squeezed the ring beneath his shirt.

The arrival of an email caused the computer to chime, and like a gong during meditation, disturbed him so the world refocused, the ceiling ascended, and the invisible intruders vaporized. Returned to life, he took deep breaths to calm himself, then looked at his screen. The sender was LG. She had cc'd DeLucca. A meeting at eight PM to discuss his work breakdown structure to fit in a new requirement: a forward–facing camera for gauging player response.

He forgot about Dharma's message.

#

"It doesn't make sense to do this now," Kartar said to Theckla, filling her in on the meeting from the night before. He taped the stickies on the wall, brand new stories derived from the brand new requirements.

Theckla stared keenly at him, rather than the stories. "You really do look a lot like Elvis, you know. The first week of November is an Elvis impersonators' convention. You have to go! You could use the Halloween contest for practice."

Kartar stared. How could so much be the same, yet people could keep surprising him? Although they had two years of document review meetings behind them, he'd only ever known a thin slice of Theckla, never learning she made doodads with a 3D printer, collected posters from Cowboy Beebop—some Japanese cartoon, and had a BA in art. Waterfall meetings were predefined and confined by the process. With Agile, they worked harder brainstorming and problem solving instead of documenting. They worked to resolve issues guided by the Agile Manifesto and its principles. And while they did this, they shared themselves, bit by bit.

J was right. Focusing on documentation made their work all about paper rather than software. Once an initial draft filled with details was created, it had a persistence. A change required pushing and challenging the author, a conflict they'd consciously or subconsciously avoided by changing as little as possible. Now, they worked together in preparing for each Sprint by writing user stories on sticky notes. Little time was spent writing and rewriting documents. A lot of time was spent talking, thinking, and coding. With user stories, imagination and understanding created closure whereas with specifications, creativity was discouraged because re–work was expensive.

"—Kartar!" Theckla clapped her hands. "Earth to Kartar! Hey, don't take it so serious. It's just an idea." She blushed. "You'd be handsome. And if you can sing, you'd have a good chance at winning."

Kartar blushed and chose to focus on the whiteboard. Close friendships with people at work felt strange. Was this another aspect of Agile? Individuals and interactions brought people closer together because they needed each other to succeed? He nodded to himself. This time he'd get the project delivered. This time he'd make it! He had to make it because after Winner was released, he'd finally have that quiet summer with Dharma. The project was too hectic and he was working too many late nights to have her visit any earlier.

"But there's a problem," Kartar said, making a face at the row of stories stuck on the whiteboard, left to right by priority.

"You can't sing a lick?"

"No, no. Mom once flew me to audition in

Bollywood."

Her jaw dropped.

Kartar stood and placed the stories they'd planned earlier beneath the new ones.

"What do you see?"

Theckla shook her self back into the meeting. "Two different themes. We had planned on extending our simple slots into, well, simple slots with the ability to buy chips with any major credit card."

"And PayPal."

"Well yeah. We did PayPal a few Sprints ago."

"Sorta. We're blocked from integration testing until Arch and Ka–Ching enter the Development Phase. That's our other major problem."

Theckla held hands over cheeks and bounced in her chair. "You and your potentially shippable product increment. Come back down to Earth Kartar. We—"

"Sorry, back to this." He pivoted in front of the board, mimicking Vanna White, highlighting new stories with graceful gestures.

"So lovely when you do that," she said and rolled her eyes.

"Your analysis is correct! We could've finished simple slots and the ability to buy chips, next Sprint. Had Donny and Noah also done Scrum, we'd have shipped at the end of next Sprint, and Winner'd be making money. We'd have people in De'Arte using them, playing them, and spending money with them eight months earlier than the current plan!"

"Except on EARTH we're in Design AND don't have hardware AND haven't purchased the backend server."

"All solvable problems! We could've planned better! Organized our entire development staff around a . . . a vision of delivering a working product, feature by feature, over the next few months."

Kartar slapped at the new user stories. "But instead we do this." He made a face. "Implementing a forward–facing camera. Barely a glimmer of a new idea the business had. They don't even understand how to use it. Those requirements are filled with speculation!"

Near a fighter pilot's speed of reflexes, Theckla snatched her phone from the table and snapped a photo. "Sorry. You're so pouty in moments of passion. We've been trying to catch you in the act." She smiled wickedly. "The team promised to cover my coffee expenses for a month if I got a good one. There. Emailed. Give up! The information has been set free."

Kartar glared. "Have you listened to a word I've said?"

Her hands trembled, shaking the phone while she fought for self control.

He threw his hands up and spoiled the shot as her phone flashed.

"Sorry." She slid the phone to the other side of the table, out of snatching range. "Accident," she mumbled.

"Theckla!"

"They're planning on Photoshopping a sequin outfit and other things. I can't get in the way of such creativity —"

"Theckla!"

"I got what you're saying!" She wiggled fingers as if casting a spell. "It's an R&D thing. If we started over, we'd change how the business operates so things didn't suddenly go all BIG R and little D. We'd stick with little R and BIG D, and quickly deliver something to our guests. And DeLucca would patiently study how each feature caused money to roll in instead of letting the business chase the latest new hotness before they know what to do with it. I get it Kartar, I really get it. We should be executing with—"

"A single vision. You know, like other successful and innovative companies."

"Well, back in the real world, we're going to do what LG and DeLucca say." She waited for him to break the silence. Time passed. "Right Kartar? Right?"

She jumped to her feet. Her chair rolled into a wall. "Kartar! We must! It's suicide to go against LG and DeLucca!"

"Yes," he said, frowning.

#

Kartar was surprised that the team was even more upset than he and Thekla. The meeting room stayed silent after introducing the new stories.

Rockstar raised an eyebrow and looked at Prince. Prince turned at the glance and both looked at Kong, whose eyes sank to stare at the tabletop.

"What's that about?" said Theckla. None answered. "Kartar? What's this secret Dev language mean?"

Rockstar broke from reverie. "As you wish Kartar. You're the PM."

"Yeah," said Prince. "We'll just do what we're told."

Kong's head sunk. "This Agile Manifesto stuff isn't going well at all."

Kartar felt his face turning red. Theckla noticed and said, "Come on guys. Let's talk. Can it be that bad? We've Simple Slots implemented with PayPal. Now they want us to try something else."

"But—," said Prince and stopped. He rocked back, hands clamped to head and squeezed to prevent words hemorrhaging from his head.

To Kartar's amazement, it was Kong that spoke. Kong, who, during tense moments, never used words but tended toward a Bruce Lee–like impassivity. "Like in construction, we knew where the train track was headed and what we'd been asked to do. Now all of a sudden . . . ." Kong's initiative died and he closed his mouth, looking away.

Rockstar shook his head. "Now all of a sudden, we're applying wings to the caboose. Before we have tried to fire the boiler."

Kartar nodded. "But we've automated tests for all of our code—"

"Code that," Prince said, "we've never observed working with Arch and Ka–Ching." He slumped over the table, cheek to tabletop. "It's based on faith with 'nearly' working software—Yes, it's better than only doing design docs," he added as Theckla and Kartar looked upset. He lifted his head. "We even discovered and solved some problems—"

Rockstar snapped fingers together. "Precisely! Like those API changes we fed back to Kartar, who then fed them back to the other teams."

Prince shook his head. "I still think it'd be faster if we did our own architecture and backend."

"Whoa smart guy!" said Kartar. "You've never talked about that."

Prince's face became red.

Kong spoke, "We talked about it after standup because you always had your own ideas then. Hey Boss, we're good people. We do it your way." Kong shrugged. "Prince had that idea about developing our API without the backend, but you stopped him because you didn't want Daily Scrum to go too long. Then you went to all those meetings with other teams, and eventually got the same idea. You did the interfaces and documented the architecture we follow. So you decide, and we do our best. No one can get in trouble that way. Right?"

Kartar didn't nod. They had their own way of looking

at the world. It seemed unfair to complain about how he'd resolved their impediment. Maybe J would know why they behaved this way.

He pointed at the stickies on the whiteboard. "Now that that's settled, here's the Sprint Backlog. Let's play us some poker!"

Instead of leaving their seats to examine the stories, they simply stared at the stickies on the whiteboard. Not a single person picked up their cards. Rockstar leaned back and pinched his chin. Prince went back to slumping across the table. Kong squinted, sucked his lips and released them with a smack.

Theckla went to the whiteboard. "I brought the baseline stories, because Kartar keeps forgetting." She winked at her audience. "Some ScrumMaster!" On the wall she stuck baselines for story points two, four, and sixteen; stories finished in previous Sprints that the team had decide were representative of those numbers.

No one budged other than to shift, suck lips, or other various, unhelpful fidgets.

At the last planning meeting, they did it all: Like he was born to it, Kong demanded they start with estimating payment because he had new understandings from working on previous payment stories. Rockstar and Prince debated Kong's details, but when Kartar asked them to choose a poker card, and they each showed an eight, it meant their different implementation details didn't affect their capacity, as it would be the same level of effort. During the Sprint, they'd decide which implementation while under influence of the work rather than isolated in a meeting. In half an hour, they had reviewed their estimates. In the next hour, they'd written and reviewed tasks for each story, then reviewed the Sprint Plan to decide whether or not to go with it. All together, they used a total of two hours for the planning meeting.

It hadn't always been that way. In Sprint one, they'd done a traditional work breakdown structure with hours and used a project planning tool. It took a day and a half; everyone was worn out and unhappy. Before the next planning meeting, Kartar read a dozen webpages of advice and bought Planning Poker cards and sticky notes. With those tools, they finished in half a day, and everyone agreed the meeting moved faster with stickies and a wall than trying to use a laptop and projector. After reading webpages concerning a process called Backlog Grooming, they held a one–hour meeting two days before Sprint Planning to see if the next Sprint's stories were 'planning ready' using UTES—Understandable, Testable, Estimatable, and Small enough. Using the two days before Sprint Planning, Theckla and Kartar resolved many of the problems that had failed the UTES test. So Sprint Backlog grooming brought Sprint Planning down to less than two hours! That night, Prince had helped Kartar produce a YouTube video of him burning his Art of Waterfall series. Dharma saw it and called him—by voice—to declare him a cool YouTube dad!

Having the team run the meetings had reduced meeting duration by more than 50%. Today however . . . .

"OK," Kartar said. "Let's start with the hardware driver story. The business wants us to add a forward–facing camera so they're able to see the guest as they play."

The three just looked at each other then back at Kartar.

He said, "What do you think?"

The three shrugged. Kartar rolled his eyes, exasperated.

"Come one guys! What's all this . . . ."

"What's all of what?" said Prince.

"Shrugs and— Hell, what happened to the team from

a few weeks ago?"

Kong broke first. "Maybe we need to get some BRDs and Requirements docs."

Theckla's eyes widened like he'd sprouted a horn. "You want to go back to—"

Prince, his face turning red, said "These camera stories! Why do they want it? What's the point?"

Rockstar jumped in. "The project seems to be wandering Kartar. Why a camera all of a sudden?"

Kartar frowned. "Why does it matter? Just give the estimates and build—"

Prince groaned. Kong's face became impassive. Rockstar slapped palm to forehead. "Bugger all! It does matter. We design better software when we know how it will be used. Because we can't see where Winner is headed, it is like every direction is wrong."

Kong snapped to standing. "It's like we hike Taishan mountain during a fog. Will we arrive at the temple or fall off a cliff? No one knows!"

Kartar looked at Theckla who raised her eyebrows with a slight head shake, her meaning clear: "Don't look at me, I don't know what the business wants."

"Can't we just implement something simple?"

"What's simple for this case?" said Rockstar. "Is it black and white? Is it one megapixel? A thousand? How can we know where to start when the business hasn't told us what it wants to do with it?"

Prince snapped his fingers. "Maybe it's infrared? You know, just a motion sensor."

"Is the lens fixed or variable focus?" said Kong.

Kartar took a seat, nodding with them. LG and DeLucca weren't ready, and they were forcing him to pass on the uncertainty to the team. The camera could be the simple expression one from his first life, or it could be the innovative, first ever, emotion tracking system from his second. And, of course, it could always be entirely different this time around too.

Kartar paced in front of the whiteboard, thinking on how involved he'd been in forming the project vision with Debbie and J, how clear he'd been with the importance of each requirement. He'd passed the hot potato.

"Theckla, what is it they want?"

Theckla took a deep breath. "A camera that can identify the player."

"Why?"

"I'm not sure. I thought we'd just stick a camera on it and—oh hell. You guys are right. That story is not ready."

"So we do it my way," Kartar said.

"That won't fly," she said. "LG said this had to start ASAP so we'd be ready when DeLucca returned from a conference."

"Cancel the Sprint until DeLucca gets back?" said Kartar.

Theckla shook her head. "A great way of getting fired!"

Rockstar said, "So this is a political pigeon! There's no point in being idealistic, a Sir Thomas More as it were. Although you won't be beheaded, you won't be canonized for your trouble either."

Everyone stared at Rockstar who looked from one face to the other, but none met his glance with understanding.

"King Henry wanted to—oh, never mind. I'm alone on a continent of ignorance." Rockstar winked and continued. "Kartar, might I offer a suggestion? We do only one camera story, scope it small. As for the rest, we continue with the other work. So we get slots done, yet still start work on the camera."

Kartar thought about his past lives, how mood tracking requirements had eventually crashed down onto them, how challenging it became to build such magic. What had worsened matters was the business's certainty it could be done in a few weeks, based on some vague WSJ article. He could force his team to start with vague stories based on what had happen before, but what if something changed? They'd be wasting a Sprint on guess work instead of on stories which were certain to be valuable.

He and Theckla stepped to the corner for a whispered conference.

Prince sat up. "What the heck do you think the camera's for?" His compatriots only shook their heads.

Kartar and Theckla finished. "I think Rockstar's idea might work," he announced. "Here's what we do . . . ."

By the end, the team looked less unhappy, but unhappy nonetheless. At day end, Kartar sent a report to DeLucca and LG: work on the camera had started as agreed.

#

The heat was on and Kartar had no fondness for it, not one bit. LG and DeLucca were strange about the camera story. Outside of a meeting or email, LG wouldn't discuss it. DeLucca only asked superficial questions or nodded at whatever Kartar said, and there was never time to answer Kartar's questions. Lovers Auditing started snooping around. The conference room speakerphone was always found switched–on before each Sprint Demo, which made no sense really, because why bother? He habitually emailed invites to DeLucca and LG who never bothered to show, always due to "other meetings." If Sis wanted to attend, anyone could've forwarded an invitation. There was no reason to "wiretap" the meeting.

Each Sprint, the team delivered working code—to a point. Dependencies to architecture and database were mocked so the system was never truly complete. Regardless, they accomplished a lot of "real" work with few meetings and documents, just as J said they would. But many things were horribly wrong, so seeing Sis Love in the office wasn't surprising. J said Scrum rapidly revealed impediments. Maybe Scrum also accelerated murder.

Kartar received a FedEx box from his family in India. He pulled the tab and the inside was stuffed with plantain leaves larger than a sheet of paper. The idea was crazy, but then, so was Agile. With sharpie at hand, he stared at the leaf on his desk, feeling foolish. Maybe it's some kind test of open–mindedness. He rolled his eyes, decided to give it a try anyways, and wrote:

'This is what's happening on my Scrum project . . . . '

He explained how his team's performance had dropped. How the team had stopped making their own decisions, so every day, he faced a deluge of emails. Although feeling needed was nice, email communication wasted time because they waited for his answer. Often a response caused another question, and the cycle went on and on until he called them. Or they'd bring it up at their next Daily Scrum. But because Daily Scrum was only once a day, again, things waited for him to decide.

He stopped writing. They acted like Winner was only his project! Upon the leaf he jotted the first two manifesto values:

Individuals and interactions over processes and tools
Working software over comprehensive documentation

They'd done better in building working software. And

it couldn't be said enough how huge a help Theckla had been. This was in direct contrast to before, where all interactions were perilous opportunities for change requests. But dependencies with Arch and Ka–Ching were a big problem. The team complained that mocking was extra work. That team . . . .

Individuals and interactions pointed to big problems with the devs. Lately, they had to be managed as before: weekly one–on–ones in addition to the Daily Scrum, and a meeting the day before the end of the Sprint to audit work against the Definition of Done. They really tried his patience. He'd been inventing new ways—adding processes—to help things move along. If that was the wrong approach, then what should be done?

Stumped, he flipped the leaf over and continued: 'The business changes directions . . . .' One month, it was all about slot games, Whack–a–Mole the next, then a little more on slot games, then the camera, changing direction faster than something releasable could be completed.

He stopped writing and looked at the last two manifesto values:

Adapting to change over following a plan
Customer collaboration over contract negotiation

Adapting to change is what he and Theckla did before every Sprint Planning. They took in the latest requests from LG and DeLucca, and brought them into the meeting. It worked great when the requests went in an understandable direction, but was frustrating when DeLucca was away and no one knew how to answer the team's questions. And LG seemed to think they only existed to follow her orders. So, for the most part, customer collaboration sucked. Everyone outside the team expected sign–offs as promises to deliver, and when someone wanted to add more, there was the typical struggle until their bosses ordered someone to do what they were told—Contract negotiation.

He put the sharpie down. They were batting two for four. If integration with Ka–Ching and Arch didn't go well, plus the rate of new ideas coming from the business, the team'd be buried. And after seeing Sis Love in the building, the only question was which PM they'd choose to 'push up daisies.'

Finished, he went to the restroom, opened a window, and tossed the leaf. Rather than wafting down, it gave one little wiggle then dropped like cardboard. On the ground it lay, weighed down by the problems and concerns that striped its skin in black sharpie. He squeezed the ring hanging beneath his shirt and wondered how this could possibly work. J was a godman, the best in India Ma had said. And expensive Dad had added. Fine. He'd done the stupid deed.

Afterward, he stopped at Donny's desk. Atop Donny's nose were reading glasses, and atop his forehead, sunglasses. He was typing the words 'Final draft' on his team's design specification, which was great news. They'd be entering the Development Phase soon, thank the gods!

"Donny. I hear you shoot."

The chair creaked beneath Donny's six–five linebacker frame as he straightened, closed one eye, and tilted his head like he'd misheard. "YOU shoot, Kartar?"

"I'm getting started. I have something to try out and want your opinion. Where do you go to shoot?"

"You got heat?" Donny's eyebrows reached toward his sunglasses. "This I've got to see! Yeah, I know a place. Leave at six?"

Kartar nodded.

"Can you tell me something?" Donny said. "How the hell are you getting all those requirements reviewed and design specs done without involving your team? LG is storming around in a fit trying to figure out what you're doing."

"Well, then she should come to a Sprint Review. Theckla and I've been handling those meetings. This leaves the team free to develop code."

"Aren't you doing the design first?"

Kartar mused on how to answer, because he wasn't sure what was happening on the development floor either. As far as he knew, they worked it out as needed when building something. This made it tough to document, so he'd been on his own to manufacture design documents.

Kartar said, "Of course we're doing a design first. Otherwise we'd end up with a mess." Heart beat faster. "We review as needed."

"Wow! You guys are doing some kinda magic. LG is certain you're cheating somehow."

"Did you tell her we're—"

"No, no. Mums the word for Noah and I. The other devs know something's up since they all sit on the same floor. My people complain they've way more meetings than yours."

"You know devs. Always complaining about meetings." Kartar turned to leave. "I need to go. I'm sure there's another document LG wants from the team."

Donny finger saluted. "See you at six."

Kartar just reached his desk when Theckla stepped out of the elevator and dashed over, her mouth masked behind a sheet of paper.

"What's up?" he said.

"I'm sure it's just a joke, so don't take it wrong." She dropped the paper on his desk, a picture from Star Wars, young Obi–Wan Kenobi dueling with a Sith Lord. The Sith Lord's head was Photoshopped.

"Why?! I've gone from Indian Elvis to this?"

"Sorry. You've been under a lot of stress, and well, you've pretty much done everything except coding."

"I haven't been that bad, have I?"

"When's the last time you had a Daily Scrum without cutting people off? Don't look hurt. I'm just saying . . . ." Theckla bowed, mimicking a submissive Japanese woman.

"My lord," she said and made fast exit for the elevator, grinning.

The picture's caption was 'Scrum Master' with 'Master' crossed out and penned to read, 'Scrum Lord.'

"I'd better nip this before it grows."

#

Kartar watched from behind a potted tree. The team was in their cubicles, each the image of relaxation with feet on desks, keyboards in laps, and in various poses of thinking.

Prince set keyboard aside and stretched. "I don't know guys. The design is so abstract it's hard to build what we need."

Kong's fingers rained across his keyboard in sudden inspiration. "It's OK," he said. "You get used to Kartar's design style. It's never simple. If you ask why, he always says something about how something might change." Kong sucked lips against teeth. "Always need a lot of interfaces and classes. Even for an easy thing."

Rockstar leaned into Prince's cubicle. "What if we adjusted the design in this case? An observer pattern would really simplify this Sprint's work."

"True," Prince said, sitting up and excited, then slouched. "You'll need authorization from Kartar. He's involved with all the work with Arch and Ka–Ching. We've no idea what could happen if we decide on our own."

Kong nodded. "The boss has his own ideas. Better send him an email."

Rockstar stiffened. "Do you realize how long it would take to express this to him? This is the 'micro' level in 'micromanagement.' We do this, we cut out half the work. If we do it now and show him later, it would be quite clear why it's better."

"Your funeral," said Prince. He started to play an online video game.

Rockstar didn't give up. "Chaps, have you read the Agile Manifesto principles at AgileManifesto.org? It says: Continuous attention to technical excellence and good design enhances agility. That's what I'm doing."

Kong said, "Kartar's already done that for us."

Prince's screen flashed with laser fire and destruction. "The manifesto also says to 'maximize work not done.' So that's what I'm doing—No work."

Rockstar shook his head. "That's bollocks. It says, 'Simplicity—the art of maximizing work not done—is essential.' Said another way, Kartar shouldn't have designed for every Sprint. Better to design Sprint by Sprint, incrementally. We should never build what isn't immediately needed."

Prince nodded while focused on alien destruction. "Like worrying about level ten when I'm stuck on level five."

"Right. With the automated unit tests we have, we can keep our rate of code changes high. All of which brings me back to 'continuous attention to technical excellence.' When we try a better idea, our tests tell us if there's a problem within minutes."

Kong said, "Yes. When a test fails, I just tap ctrl–Z to undo it and try something else that doesn't cause regression."

For a moment the group said nothing and watched

Prince's game play.

Kong said, "Rockstar, don't change the design. The guy who spoke to Chairmen Mao about the Great Leap Forward was giving attention to policy excellence. And you know what happened to him." At the two's silence, Kong sucked his lips. "Banished penniless to the countryside. It's the boss's project. You run everything by him or you'll get Scrum–Lorded."

From across the room LG approached. Rockstar noticed first and quickly returned to his workstation to look busy.

Kartar kept cover behind the tree. He leaned against the wall and pretended to read email on his phone as he thought about what he learned: There were some things he liked about his team's individuals and interactions, and a lot he didn't. Had he made them this way? During Daily Scurm, they kept bringing up dependency issues and wanted to talk about them further, even though he'd already resolved them. They had other ideas, like doing their own architecture and DB work, which would resolve dependency problems but was hard for other reasons, such as persuading Donny and Noah to give the work to Wow. Why couldn't his team just follow his design?

Frustrated, he banged his head against the wall. Had he taken this impediment because they needed him to, or had he done it because he wanted control? Obviously his design hadn't met their approval. Although control wasn't the same as resolving, his strategy won him both. Why should that make him a Scrum Lord?

"Whatcha doing?" said a voice nearly in Kartar's ear.

Kartar startled into the tree. The pot tipped. Donny caught the tree's trunk.

Kartar glared. "Don't do that!"

"Sorry. I sometimes stand here to see what's really going on too." Donny smiled.

"But you're the size of Mean Joe Green! This isn't enough tree!"

Donny chuckled. "A little camouflage goes a long ways. Come on. Time to go."

#

Kartar opened the Cadillac's trunk. Donny leaned close to watch Kartar move around ammo boxes and an assortment of gun–n–rifle magazines.

"Kartar! You closet gun freak! Half of this can't be legal. And what the hell is this?"

Donny lifted a headsct/mic combo with a whip–cord antenna.

Kartar snatched it away. "Careful! That's expensive! A broad–spectrum scanner."

Donny whistled. "Must be quite a bee buzzing up your skirt."

Kartar put the headset on. "See? Do I look like a real SWAT—" Herbal. The mic smelled from Donny's handling. Something herbal. With eyes closed, he whiffed again. It was same scent as what was left behind on the speakerphone!

He glanced at the trunk load of firearms, all which were loaded and organized in a foam partitioned box, then he watched Donny. Was this easygoing giant the inside man for Lovers?

He held a mental image of what was in the trunk, how the weapons were laid out and what could be grabbed and aimed in a hurry. It'd have to be the shotgun. Shaky hands wouldn't matter. Not at this range.

He pointed at Donny's hand. "Can I see your college ring?" Kartar slid in front of the trunk, putting himself between Donny and the weapons. Donny held out his hand. Kartar examined the University of Miami championship ring.

Donny said, "What's wrong? You're red all of a sudden."

Kartar sniffed the ring.

"Eww!" Donny pulled his hand away.

"You lit up a roach?"

Donny shook his head, holding hand to forehead in embarrassment. "No, it's hand lotion. Yes, it really is!"

"Sure. Whatever," Kartar said flatly.

Donny lifted his hands to surrender. "OK, Mr. DEA, you caught me. I just washed my hands. And you know, it's fall n'all. So my skin's feeling chapped. When I left the bathroom, I saw Noah had forgotten his bottle of fancy Japanese hand lotion. On his desk." He pointed at Kartar. "Look, he's really protective of it, so don't snitch. Says it's expensive. Sencha tea–based or some such nonsense. Got it off Think Geek, knowing him."

Kartar squinted at Donny's face, absorbing this new information and trying to decide if he was being lied to. Last time, it was Noah's idea to fake the Gantt chart. Noah, though a pain in the ass for sure, was a technical elitist. How could Lovers get to a guy like that?

Kartar nodded. "Alright, alright. The secret of your klepto habit is safe with me." He closed the trunk and gestured at Donny's hand. "And wow! Have you considered being a hand model?"

While Donny laughed, Kartar's phone buzzed with a message from Dharma:

'Dad, I'm in Vegas tomorrow!!! My friend's dad is an event planner and is bringing us to a Ninja's Versus Pirates convention. Come and get me!'

\#

No matter how fast Kartar sped through his inbox,

answering team questions, more appeared.

I NEED TO TAKE THE AFTERNOON OFF, Kartar put in the subject line. After sending it, another email with another detail came back. MAKE SOME DECISIONS FOR YOURSELVES!—he left that one in the drafts folder. Although a wreck at Daily Scrum, he took control and got it finished in five minutes. Afterwards, Theckla pulled him aside.

"What's with you today?"

"My daughter's in town. A surprise visit. She's over at Circus Circus. Now."

"Oh . . . . I see." Theckla rested her hand on his arm. "Take the afternoon off."

"Theckla, the team needs me to help them with—"

"It's OK. The project will be here when you return."

"But they're going to get blocked. They get blocked on everything now! There's this mechanic I need to talk to. I must have done something wrong."

Theckla's gaze wandered to the left, to the right, to the ground, then back up. "Go see your daughter. It'll be good for you."

It's all I live for—Kartar thought.

"Here," she said, removing a bracelet from her wrist. "You need to give her a gift. Tell her you had it made."

Stunned, he looked at the florescent neon strands of reds, blues, and pinks woven together in his hand. Tiny lightsabers, blasters, and Stormtrooper helmets dangled from the bracelet.

"Dharma knows about Star Wars, right?"

"Come on! She's my daughter. That's a broadsword lightsaber, isn't it?"

"What do you think? Think she'll like it?"

He couldn't speak. Her phone made a rude noise, making her glance at it. "Oh, gotta go! Auditors visiting."

"Depressing." Head shake. Everything was happening

too fast. "It's not even Thanksgiving."

Theckla's eyebrows twisted in puzzlement. "I'm talking auditors, not pilgrims. What does Thanksgiving— Just go see your daughter." As she left, waves of dizziness struck him, one after another, and coming fast. He clung to the nearest cubicle as exotic incense and the sound of chanting in an ancient language swept over him.

His phone pinged. Back pressed against the wall, he glanced at its face and swore. Chanting faded to the hissing sound of the janitor spraying freshener at the water fountain, obliterating all traces of ancient India with the overpowering scent of artificial lemon.

DeLucca wanted to see him.

#

Kartar squatted beside his car and used the glow of his phone to check underneath for foreign objects—bombs, bugs, etc. A transmitter was adhered beneath the back bumper, Lovers' favorite hiding place. He relocated it where it would look best: LG's Lexus. Sadly, the rearrangement imparted no pleasure. LG had really screwed him. Perhaps fatally.

He drove out of the garage and slowly entered the street. No ad–wrapped vans, yet. He accelerated. The charm bracelet lay in the other seat, looking perfectly ready to wrap around his beautiful girl's wrist. It was all façade however. Everything was going to hell. Everything.

DeLucca's voice, how cold it sounded while he barked that Kartar was fucked, that LG had outed him to Lovers Auditing, that Kartar hadn't followed their process, and no way the sponsors would let Kartar leave without 'an accounting' for 'grossly negligent' decisions. The deadly issuance that came from DeLucca didn't stop, no matter how much assurance Kartar gave that team Wow was on schedule. Kartar tried to explain, as J had taught, how what Donny and Noah did hid problems for the future, but DeLucca cut him off.

He proceeded the few blocks to Circus Circus. He'd go through with seeing Dharma. Because of the fluke of restarting life twice, it'd been a year and a half since he'd seen her face, heard her laugh, or kissed her forehead. Her hair would smell of something tropical from The Body Shop.

"See her for a few minutes. Say, 'hi.' And then leave her to go into hiding."

He parked, went inside, and saw the pirates first: men and women dressed in ostentatious pantaloons with colorful head scarves and sashes, bejeweled scabbards with plastic or foam swords swinging from their hips. Tall pirates, short pirates, fat pirates, pirate toddlers, every type of buccaneer was flashing costume jewelry and bright colors during the walk to the cavernous playground that was the Adventuredome. Software pirates with USB bangles, DVD pirates with sashes buckled by shiny disks, even a mattress pirate with a shirt made from tags labeled 'Do not remove!' Towering above it all were roller coasters, air drop rides, and other spinning, tossing, and churning amusements set among faux desert towers and jungle trees. The density of eye patches increased with each step until climaxing at the Sand Pirate ride, whose boat launch was established as 'Pirate HQ.' He stood out of the way beside a faux jungle tree and contemplated the buccaneers while massive hydraulics swung the pirate boat higher and higher. Pirates everywhere and only pirates.

He said to himself, "Why can't I find the ninjas?"

"Dad!" Someone hooked his waist from behind. Another had his leg. He pried the arms loose and spun to face his assailants.

"Dad!"

It took only an instant. "Dharma!"

Two short ninjas, only their eyes left uncovered by black jumpsuit. Within one he sensed a familiar smile.

She said, "We really had you—"

He leapt forward and lifted the startled ninja into the air before she could retreat. Although trapped, she wrapped arms around his neck then pulled his head against hers. Cheek to cheek, warmth spread between them in a moment of love that he wished would last an eternity. Against his face was the softness of hers and the dampness of tears.

"Uh. Dad. OK. Please put me down now. You're embarrassing me."

"Oh, sure. Right." He lowered his little girl to the floor, thinking she'd grown so much over the year. Nonsense. For this reality, he'd left Bay Area only months ago.

From behind a potted plant appeared a thin adult ninja who companionably pulled the other short ninja alongside. The adult extended his hand.

"Hi Mr. Patel, I'm Asim Hanson, your daughter's neighbor. It's great to meet you. She talks about you all the time."

They shook hands. A commotion of people and voices rang out—"NINJAS!"

"Come on Dad!" His three–quarter sized ninja daughter pulled him along.

They fled. Kartar ran, following his daughter through the attraction center, past the swinging ship, past fronds of plants and trees growing at the foot of desert towers. Pirates were everywhere, chasing after them, pushing through crowds, shouting "avasts" and "args" and various threats regarding planks. Ahead, a double row of potted shrubbery escorted a line of yellow duct tape that crossed the floor in both directions. They crossed the demarcation and followed a path that wound between faux jungle trees. An arrow–shaped sign of knotty wood indicated their destination was a dance club. Written on paper taped to the arrow was, 'NINJAS!' Another sign pointed back the way they came. Written on its paper was 'PIRATES!'

They entered a mockup village of shanties with jungle patterned paper walls and curved bamboo rooftops. Barrels of provisions surrounded a dance floor turned into a village square. House music boomed from barrels, strobes and lasers flashed and swept overhead.

The place looked abandoned.

Kartar halted at a barrel atop which half–finished drinks remained. He gasped for Dharma to stop, his body rebelling from unexpected exercise. Why must they run from overweight pirates? Although it was Vegas, it wasn't an alternate reality. What could happen?

A mob of pirates formed at the border. Most honored the division and taunted them from the other side of the line as "ninja sissies." Three lady pirates approached, long black hair streaming back, gold sashes across their chest upon which was written "Bangkok Mateys." Their leader, a beauty with a gold ring looped through one nostril, ordered Kartar to "submit" as they charged into the village, sequined pantaloons shimmering with each stride.

Kartar shielded Dharma with his body as the dark–eyed beauties closed in. The leader, black lipstick and eyeshadow highlighting her already striking features, billowy shirt glowing in the club's light, swung at him, her arm moving in slow–mo under the strobe light. He jerked back then realized it was her hand rather than a saber. She was trying to tag him.

Dharma shouted and stepped beside Kartar; her hand

wound back, gripping a throwing star. With a flick, she struck the pirate's chest. The star should have punctured the woman between "Bangkok" and "Mateys," but bounced off harmlessly. The air was suddenly filled with missiles blown, launched, or thrown from dark shadows behind barrels of provisions and from rooftops. The "Mateys" were struck several times; soft stars, Nerf darts, and soft nunchucks littered the floor.

"Argggg!" yelled the leader, lowering hands in defeat. "I'd've had him with me saber. Next time Elvis."

"Yeah, next time," the others mumbled. "Cross over to our side where we can use our weapons." "Cowards!" yelled another.

The Mateys rejoined the host on the other side of the line.

Asim stood up from behind a barrel. "Good Lord! I thought they had us that time!"

Dharma turned around. "See Dad? Even they call you Elvis!"

Asim and his daughter laughed.

Kartar turned to reply but surprise stole response. Before, where there had been only house music and abandoned drinks, were ninjas toasting each other and dancing. The pirate horde dwindled to their side of the theme park.

He thanked Asim, then joined his daughter at a barrel set for two. They talked over faux wood mugs of root beer, face–to–face for the first time since before he was gunned down in the desert. Around them, ninjas from short to tall socialized over drinks, threw darts, and break danced to house.

"I have something for you." He slipped the bracelet from his pocket and wrapped it around his daughter's wrist.

Dharma gasped once for each charm she examined.

"Dad! I love it!"

She sprang from her seat and hugged him, practically in his lap like when she was six. They held each other, Kartar collapsed forward on his stool, Dharma bent backwards and up. They sat hugging together that way, father and daughter, sharing a moment important enough for an eternity, yet not lasting long enough at all, while all around the two, ninjas broke into mock battle. Black figures made impossible leaps across village rooftops, and higher up, more flew at each other on near–collision courses, harnessed to rollercoaster tracks re–purposed for skyhook battles.

"Skyhook battles?" Kartar said.

"Sure Dad. Come! I'll show you. Don't be such a scaredy–cat."

#

Kartar arrived home just after midnight. Tired, he mis–steered the big caddy's entry into the small garage, backed out to re–angle, then got the car to fit the whole way. After turning ignition off, he closed eyes and relived the warmth of Dharma's hug. How she'd grown! She was excited to stay for the summer. But seven months was so far away!

And already Winner spiraled out of control. LG had outed him, and it was anybody's guess if Donny and Noah would help throw him to the wolves. And Noah, as improbable as it seemed, was working with the wolves.

Any moment now, Sis and Lex would make their move.

He'd do anything to make it to summer, to see Dharma. Going into hiding wouldn't work. They might kill his entire family. On Monday, he'd find a way to get actual WORKING software as his team wanted: without mocks and stubs. He'd make Donny and Noah help somehow. He'd get it done if he had to do it all himself: design, coding, and test. Switching the bedroom light on, he removed his clothes. Sitting on the bed in socks, underwear, and undershirt, he noticed emails from the team who waited for him to handle everything.

"Shit!"

He curled fingers into fists and squeezed, arms shaking, whole body quivering. Although his team came to work, they'd abandoned him. Kong and Prince did only exactly what he told them to. Rockstar had all but gone underground. Because he'd designed the interfaces to Arch and Ka–Ching, he was the wheel of the project, and the spokes had begun to resent him.

Like a boneless doll, he flopped backward onto the sheets. He tapped phone to forehead, attempting to shake loose memories of how upset Prince became when asked 'not waste time' on something Kartar would handle. He'd used that line too many times.

"Yes," he said out loud and recited in the tone of desperate self–realization heard at AA meetings, "I am a Scrum Lord."

Because he handled everything, they handled nothing. The Daily Scrum had become a perfunctory status report. As he had learned when spying on the team, they actively filtered out problems they didn't want him party to. They didn't trust him. He'd taken away the team's authority, and now problems snowed him under.

He must allow them to drive the resolution of the dependency problem with Noah and Donny. If he was to succeed, he must give them the support and trust needed to get the job done. There wasn't any other way.

He would make the PM floor the same as the development floor, as J had suggested. Had he done that, he'd have detected this problem earlier. Fix the first manifesto value, and he'd be three for four.

Come back to the light, oh Scrum Lord. But what about 'customer collaboration over contract negotiation?' He thought back to when he had ever collaborated with a customer . . . Firefly.

With Firefly, the business owner sat with him and J. When he'd thought of CRM and a complicated website, Debbie was present to clarify business goals, which J wrote as a user story. Debbie had been an integral part of the planning. Whereas with DeLucca, the ideas he received from other directors manifested themselves in email via LG, who passed it on to Theckla—typical Waterfall style planning. Email, the shaky wooden bridge of collaboration, was what the business relied on.

That wasn't the only problem. With Winner, the business's foremost belief was they had a year to finish everything they could dream up, and because they weren't actively collaborating, the team got new requirements that no one fully understood. With Firefly, they'd committed to releasing in the very near future. This forced each Sprint to be building blocks that served the release. They quickly discarded ineffective ideas for effective solutions that could be released on time: the poster and SMS idea. But how to get DeLucca collaborating with his team? How to break free from the Waterfall determined to drag him over the precipice no matter how hard he swam against the current?

He closed his eyes and said, "I want to break free." The Queen song playing over his speakers resonated while he contemplated the Scrum process J'd drawn. He needed something to help with organizing the Product Backlog. Something that'd draw DeLucca out of his office. Something that transformed vague business ideas into building blocks that could be released frequently and incrementally. Something that actually influenced what got on the Product Backlog. But where was that godman when you needed him? Ma spent good money yet all Kartar could do was write essays on leaves and do his own research.

With his phone he searched the web for Scrum, Product Backlog, and planning. In the middle of reading a promising article about 'Five Levels of Planning,' the phone went dead.

Give up for the night, he decided. The five levels could wait for morning. He felt in the gap between the bed and wall and found his forty–five auto a bit out of place. He nudged it back into position and turned off the light.

Eyes closed and comfortable until—he had no alarm. The phone was dead. And the charging cable wasn't bedside where it was supposed to be.

It was in the car. He groaned then cursed himself for forgetting to buy another on the way home. He'd left his working one at the office.

Through the dark house he returned to the garage, snapped on the light, and walked to the car door, socks poor protection against the chilly cement floor.

Opening the door was loud in the quiet. He leaned across the driver's seat and grabbed the cable. From inside the house, a floor creaked.

After today's meeting with DeLucca starring his own office window, he was taking no chances. His pistol left beside the bed was no longer a factor. Leaving his phone charging on the seat, Kartar popped the trunk and slipped on night vision goggles, radio scanner earwig, then paused to decide between the Mac 10, AR 15, and the pump action sawed–off shotgun. He picked up the shotgun then stared at a pair of grenades. No pockets for them, and quite frankly, they were scary. He left them where they lay.

The scanner picked up a mobile signal and before hearing a voice, he knew trouble had come: gaelic sounding strings, flutes, and drums. Irish step music in the background, as clear as day.

"Housekeeper, are ya finished dearie?"

Kartar ducked behind the car as tears filled his eyes— Lex!

Sis responded, "Almost. But kitty got up and left the bedroom. You see him out back?"

"Nay, backyard's empty. Going to the front."

Then silence. Kartar got the phone and pressed the power button. And waited. LED blinked, then logo came up. His fingers poised to strike 911.

They continued talking without wasting words: "Side of house clear, moving to front," "Second bedroom clear, going to hallway," and "Broom closet clear, still no movement." Although the words were innocuous, the tone was intense, like the Daily Scrum before he screwed them up. A bit of status—just enough to signal problems. No, not just to signal problems, but to also coordinate supporting activities. Right now, he couldn't trust his team to find a lost puppy. Lovers took extreme ownership of their work. As for his phone, it showed the Blackberry symbol, slowly getting brighter. Almost there. On the scanner: "I see light inside the garage."

He rushed to the wall and snapped off the overhead light. In spite of that—gods, the trunk light! He scrambled, stubbed a toe, recovered balance, then limped to and closed the lid. Panting, he activated night vision and flipped the scope before his shooting eye. The world went from black to amber green.

Scanner: "Light off—"

"Yeah, I heard something," Sis replied.

"Move or no?"

"Holding. Go back to position A for support."

"Nay, move! Maybe the kitty ran. I've got the front. Chase kitty to me."

"Moving."

More noise upstairs, quick footsteps down carpeted stairs. They closed in. Lex waited outside. Sis inside. He needed a wild card.

He opened the trunk, its light blinding an eye in brilliant green. He took a grenade and slammed the lid shut. The door to the house, still unmoving. Good. He needed his team so motivated. He needed them dedicated to Winner like the Lovers were so dedicated to killing.

Scanner: "Light in garage. On–n–off. Strange. The hell's kitty doing?"

"At door, listening."

While watching the door, he grabbed the phone from the front seat, and with grenade in one hand, dialed 911 with the other.

"911 Operator, what's the nature of your—"

The door swung open into the garage. He dropped the phone, pulled the grenade pin, lifted the lever, and tossed it over the caddy's hood, at the doorway. It arced at the green amber woman. It flew by her legs, not touching and unnoticed by Sis. She entered just as the grenade knocked against the hallway wall. Sis dropped to a crouch beside the car front. The grenade bounced back into the garage. It dropped down each step, thud, thud, thud. And stopped near the woman.

"Gods no," Kartar cried. Into the car he dove where he curled into the footwell and prayed.

The car blew into the air. Heat, pain, then nothing.

PRODUCT VISION

For the fourth excruciating time, Kartar sat in the same project startup meeting with LG, Theckla, Noah, and Donny. It was terrible enough being shot in the desert, executed on the monorail, and then blown up by a grenade. But also made to suffer the same meeting four times? This had to be some new definition of Hell.

They discussed all the exciting new opportunities the Winner would bring the casino. The project managers were excited, the BAs were excited, everyone smiling, animated, and engaged . . . everyone except Kartar.

It's not going to work the mantra went through his mind while the PMs debated how to separate work between the teams. It's not going to work, the conclusion twisted his gut as LG and Theckla discussed the advanced state the requirements and BRDs were in. It's not going to WORK—the knowledge shook his being while the group transitioned from seemingly stable documentation to the topic of timeline and milestones. None of them saw they were already doomed. Everything would change: schedule, costs, requirements. The perfect project plans, the perfect Gantt charts, the perfectly planned engineer hours, days, and months were beautiful to look at—Now. Within days, the changes would start to happen, and within a month, all that beautiful and perfect documentation would be false. A lie. But, at this moment, they believed all of it. And he was damned to live this over and over again. Someone once said, do the same thing repeatedly and expect something else to happen although it never does, then you should be fitted for a straight–jacket.

"I'm going to get some water," said Kartar and left the room before he started to rave. In the hallway, a flood of sensation from another place swept over reality: rhythmic drumming pulsed against him, chanting voices ruffled hair, and thick incense overcame the smell of deodorized office carpet. It was as if he'd entered a temple. He forced himself to keep walking, doing his best to ignore how his skin tingled. It became difficult to see the beige office walls as his vision shimmered and shrank to a tunnel. Knees felt weak. The floor underfoot felt insubstantive, like walking on forest loam. Shouldn't the water fountain be here?

A brahma bull brushed pass, lumbering the opposite direction. Off balance, Kartar bumped into something— the water fountain, which meant he was beside the elevator. Hoping it would bring him back to some semblance of reality, he slapped the button and blindly sought the water stream, desperate as anyone lost seeking succor. Refrigerated water splashed between lips and down chin, his vision clearing. He straightened and marveled at what just had happened.

The Indian fables Ma loved to parrot always had explanations and lessons attached to them. The law of dharma, also known as karma, declared that our condition in life was the result of actions during previous lives.

Although he'd always believed these Hindu tales were told to children to get them to behave, something had definitely been happening to him, for four lives now. He'd made Winner the center of his life. And still hadn't succeeded.

Water wasn't adequate enough to shake him entirely from the spell, so he continued down the hall to get a latte, ruminating. The first time, he'd tried to change how they planned the project. But no matter how good the requirements were, someone always came up with something better, and Waterfall just couldn't keep up. It was a slowly unwinding disaster.

During the first Sprint with J to deliver value to their PO within hours instead of years, J had changed him. The mechanic had been judgmental, kind, and genuinely wanted to help Winner. If Lovers hadn't interrupted, they would've delivered something of value in ninety minutes. Quick delivery drove change in every step of the process: planning, execution, and completion. During his last life, he'd changed Wow's planning and ignored the source of the plans. He'd only changed his team's execution, even though Winner required all three.

He'd changed too little!

Although the coffee stand was in sight, Kartar did an an about–face and returned the way he'd come, rejoining the meeting with new passion.

Donny waved his sunglasses. "Hey Kartar, has anyone ever told you that you look like Elvis?"

Theckla nodded, dangly earrings swinging, their suspended charms she'd printed in De'Arte's colors spelling the words "WINNER."

"Yes," she said. "An Indian Elvis. It's the pompadour." "Very handsome," she assured.

The others "oohed" at the remark and she blushed.

Kartar blushed too. "Ahem. What if we had to deliver

the project in three months?"

The room became silent. Everyone stared, looking confused.

"Impossible," said Noah.

Donny yanked sunglasses from his forehead and used them to tap each ear, examining the frames like they'd affected his hearing.

"LG, how would you and DeLucca feel if we did?"

LG looked at the documents, then at him. "It's not a relevant question since you couldn't."

Kartar nabbed her requirements document. "Pen please." Stunned, LG pulled a red pen from her curly hair and handed it over. "Let's see." He flipped through the pages he'd read over and over again during past lives. Marked a few locations. And turned the document back to her.

He showed what he'd marked. "How about in the first month, we delivered a super simple slot, with one wheel say, and then over the next two months, we added more wheels along with PayPal payments. Could the business use that?"

LG's face flushed to the same color as her hair. "What are you saying? We need ALL of this done."

"Of course. And it's all very important, and all are 'must haves,' I know. But let's think about this. Within three months, could you start earning money with a Winner that functioned as a simple slot machine?"

LG said nothing; Kartar kept quiet to let the words sink in.

Theckla shook herself as if waking from a dream. "Of course! We could start making a little money now, and let development continue with the bigger project."

Noah slammed hands on the table, "But—"

Kartar raised his hand to stop him. "Let's address how we can test and build the system and hardware later. First,

I want to talk about the idea of incremental delivery to establish if there's value there, and after that, how to collaborate with the business this way.

"Because," Kartar nodded to LG, "if we can't make DeLucca happy, it doesn't matter what we decide in this room."

LG rapped on the table. "OK, you have my attention. Yes, Kartar. I don't need accounting to tell me that we could make a sizable return on the project if it launched in three months instead of waiting twelve before the project hit the ground."

"Exactly," said Kartar, ignoring groans from Donny and Noah. "We deliver early, with a minimal but marketable feature set. Get it in the hands of players who will spend money playing games and not only will it generate revenue, we'll have a feedback mechanism to guide our feature development each month.

"Otherwise," Kartar shook his head and pointed at LG's requirements document. "We're just guessing."

LG blushed as if caught in a lie.

"And," Kartar said, "whenever the business has new ideas, we simply add them into our next month's plan."

Donny slammed sunglasses on the table. Both he and Noah glared at Kartar like he was a traitor. "How? How can we deliver anything in three months?"

Kartar straightened upright as much as possible to Donny's six–four frame. "By delivering a working product every four weeks."

The room exploded into noise.

#

Kartar was alone in DeLucca's office while the old man shouted, ranted, and raved. Spit flew out every few words and DeLucca's face was as red as a gambler's balance sheet. He pounded fist on his desk, then pounded the wall, each impact skewing the hanging pictures of he and Justin Bieber drinking mojitos at the pool and of him playing poker with Taylor Swift.

"I can't fucking believe it! You got stones of steel. Kartar, where have you been all my life? I've never seen anyone come up with a plan of making something as expensive and complicated as this start earning its keep so quickly."

It was strange seeing him simultaneously raving and in a good mood. Come to think of it, he was the same when furious.

"You may be a genius," DeLucca said, raising his hand, his arm straight, making a finger gun for a shot between Kartar's eyes.

"Everyone's pretty freaked out, but they know deep down in their pinhead IT brains that what you said makes sense. Yet they don't believe."

Kartar shifted from the aim of DeLucca's finger. "That's why we need to show working software—potentially shippable software—after each Sprint so we believe it ourselves."

"Kartar, this place is filled with ears. The stakeholders will learn about this. I'm about to get on the phone with them, and if I tell them about what we're planning. You damn well better deliver. They'll fucking love it! But if all this falls apart, they'll be disappointed, and these are Vegas old timers. They'll want a pound of flesh for every ounce of letdown."

The sick feeling returned, the same he got whenever the Lovers were in the office in their expensive clothes and unnaturally heavy designer bags. How the hell was he going to pull this off?

DeLucca leaned forward, eyes squeezed into a squint. He stared hard like seeking lies or inconsistencies. His face so close, the smell of cologne became atmosphere. Nostrils expanded with an inhale, then contracted as a wave of Scotch–tainted breath brushed against Kartar's face.

"Shall I make that phone call Kartar? Can you fucking deliver?"

Gods no, Kartar opened his mouth to say. The cover of Wired, a faded and tired dream given up two deaths ago. Jumping off this train to Hell was impossible. DeLucca would never let him. All that mattered was seeing Dharma grow up.

"Yes!" Kartar shouted, sure that flecks of spit landed on DeLucca's face.

DeLucca clapped hands, nearly catching Kartar's nose, sealing fate in a cosmic bang. DeLucca danced a little, laughing, his head hanging back. A mad man.

A tingling invaded Kartar's body and he felt lightheaded, like something tugged at his soul. A barbed hook had him in the gut and dragged him toward some other place, further from where he wanted to be. Something was wrong.

Kartar snatched the lowball off the desk and gulped the Scotch. It warmed its way down and although the bad feeling eased, it'd return in full if something wasn't fixed.

He grabbed the collar of his dancing boss, stopping DeLucca's antics. He leaned close, staring the boss in the eye, thinking about what else hadn't gone well, what problems would trap him, who would eventually throw him under the bus and get him buried in the desert. "And you and LG need to come to the demo each Sprint so everyone takes it seriously. And . . ."

He paused, loosening his grip on DeLucca's shirt, instincts rebelling at this skating on thin ice, this issuance of demands. But things had to change. There must be a way to a different outcome. You can't keep doing the same things and expect different results, J had said. People don't truly collaborate unless they need each other to survive, he had said. Did DeLucca need the Winner to survive? Or was DeLucca merely interested?

"And what?" shouted DeLucca, nose inches from Karter's, nostrils flaring then contracting, sniffing for weakness, smelling hesitance.

Kartar said, "Why do you care about the Winner?" A strange look came over DeLucca's face. "What do you have to gain with this launch?"

DeLucca's eyes narrowed. Judging, Kartar realized, judging whether or not to divulge a secret. So there was something, and that meant everything would be—

DeLucca's voice lowered to a whisper. "Kartar." DeLucca looked around, as if there could be an eavesdropper. "Let's just say that a President of Casino Operations can always move to a bigger casino. Or even an acquisition could happen, if Winner injects new life into this place. Speaking hypothetically, of course."

Kartar nodded. Everything would be OK. DeLucca needed Winner to succeed too.

Kartar sat in the plush guest chair. "You have to do something for us. We want your feedback, no matter how tough. Because if you don't, we're all fucked."

"Yes!" DeLucca said and slapped Kartar's back. "Yes! You're the first IT weenie who seems to understand business! Yes! Yes, I accept! You and I, Kartar. You and I! We pull this off, we'll be as rich as fuck!"

Kartar's heart hammered while DeLucca beat his own chest like a caveman dressed in Armani.

#

'Ninjas V Pirates. What's that all about?' Kartar texted to Dharma while waiting for Donny and Noah to arrive.

'How do you know about that? Are you and mom talking again?' Dharma wrote back.

He paused to think through what he was about to do: at project start again, high stress, spearheading Agile before DeLucca. Bringing Dharma in now was a lot to balance and he'd never tried that before. But he needed to see her. 'I know the courts are sorting things out, but talk to your mom. Come stay with me before school starts.'

He looked at the time. Donny and Noah were fifteen minutes late. In the Waterfall days, he'd return to his desk because missing one meeting was a spit into the ocean; no noticeable impact. In fact, canceled meetings were often a blessing because you could return to your workstations and catchup on email, documentation, or coding. But they needed to discuss how to organize teams now to have something potentially shippable and working in four weeks, the deadline starting yesterday after his meeting with DeLucca. Just like his Sprint with J, every day counted.

Neither Donny nor Noah answered his call.

He combed his fingers through his pompadour and sighed. "OK, I'll find you."

Donny was in his cubicle, hunched over his phone and playing Angry Birds.

"Just a sec. I'll come to your desk. Later. Going for a high score. Bought a bald eagle."

But the way his eyes drifted down to the game wasn't convincing. Then the pigs won.

"Come on," said Kartar. "Let's find Noah and get to work."

Donny slipped phone into pocket and followed silently.

They found Noah at the espresso stand, debating with Rockstar the merits of functional versus procedural programming.

Kartar asked, "What happened to our meeting?"

"Got to go," Noah said to Rockstar. "We've got a 'Mission Impossible' to plan."

Kartar ignored the bait and led them into a meeting room.

Before the door clicked shut Donny spoke up. "I don't know about you, Noah, but I feel betrayed."

Kartar dropped into a seat. The two perched on the table above him.

Donny set hand atop Noah's shoulder, his head wagging in disappointment while speaking only to him: "You wouldn't go behind your fellow PMs' backs and talk to management to plan the project on your own—No, don't! Let me finish!"

Kartar closed his mouth and just listened. He'd never seen the big man so angry.

"We'd finished the BRD and requirements for a year–long project, and then you go and tell them we're going to deliver in three months?"

"Et tu Brutue," said Noah, grasping an invisible dagger and stabbing Donny. "Sticking your fellow PMs in the back for personal gain. And it's not going to work Kartar. It's all going to crash at your feet."

Kartar nodded. "You're right."

Donny and Noah turned to each other with eyebrows raised.

"I did it for my own gain. I got the project planned differently, because what we had planned couldn't work. And now, as you say, it will be on me if the project fails because I want to do something different from certain failure."

Donny said, "I don't see certain—"

"Three months! We need to release a product in three months and you are both upset because you can't see how it could be possible. You're right!"

Donny and Noah looked confused as Kartar continued.

"You're absolutely right! It won't work unless we work differently. And we've got two tries to figure out how."

Noah and Donny looked at each other, then back at Kartar, both saying, "Two tries?"

Noah said, "WDIWT? You told DeLucca we're releasing in three months!"

Again, Kartar went over how they could employ four-week Sprints, where each Sprint delivered working software.

"So you can see, we've got two rehearsals to get the quarterly release 'right,' but we need to reorganize our teams and change what we perceive as productivity to do this." Kartar looked hard at Donny and Noah. "We need to overhaul how we handle requirements, how we think of architecture, and how we work together. We won't succeed with this project using the Waterfall software development lifecycle. That I can promise you."

"Yeah," Donny said. "It's a problem." He looked at Noah who only shrugged. "OK wise guy, so what are we gonna do?"

#

Kartar talked on his earwig while twisting cinnamon sprinkled dough into French twists.

"Ma, I've been having weird dreams."

"You've always been having such imagination. You've been blessed with a muhurtha of such energies. . . ."

This wasn't going to go the right way, so he changed tact.

"But Ma, I'm in trouble. I keep reliving the same

twelve months of my life."

The line was silent.

"Ma?"

"How many times?"

"This is the fourth."

Silence drew on for ten, twenty, forty seconds—"Did you tell me about this? In your other lives?"

"No."

"This is the first? What? You don't trust your mother? Was I so cruel to you that you hide your metaphysical life from me? You treat your mother with the same trust as a stranger—"

"Ma! The problem is—"

"Sure, give your poor mother a call when you have a prob—"

"Ma, they're killers. They won't stop coming after me unless I deliver my project."

Silence, then Ma took a breath. "Have you seen anyone strange? Perhaps a bearded, old man? Someone who could be a rishi?"

"Yeah. About that. You hired a godman to help me. Just before I was killed the first time. But he's actually an 'Agile' consultant, a type of really annoying IT consultant who never answers the whole question. His name is J and he didn't leave a number, and I need to talk to him. He asked me to send messages using plantain leaves. But the leaves aren't getting me answers."

Ma was silent for once, seeming to absorb all he said. But even in her silence, he knew what she prepared to say, so before she started he said, "Don't bother telling me this is the work of an ancient Hindu sage or demigod."

"Rishis walk among us! Don't turn your back on your gotra!"

"You don't happen to have his phone number?"

"How could I? You told me I contacted him in July and that's the future. Your father and I aren't planning to go to India until next summer. But worry not. You're in his gotra! He will control time and space until you learn what you need to learn. You should try to contact him through your dreams. If you drink the right tea and chant before sleep—"

Kartar prepared to say something regrettable, but didn't because Dharma had entered the kitchen.

"Dad! Why do I smell something baking?"

He waved for her to sit. "Dharma's here Ma. Yes, I worked out a deal with Lisa to have her over until school starts. I've got to run. Love you, and she sends her love too. Bye."

He slid a sheet of chocolate croissants out of the oven and transferred them onto a dish, reloading the sheet with cinnamon twists.

Dharma gaped at the pastries. "You're a chef all of a sudden?"

He handed her a plate with a cooling croissant, a fruit tart, and a sprig of mint. "First you complain how hard it was to find French butter. Now, will you complain on these properly flaking pastries?"

She opened her mouth and Kartar plugged it with the croissant. "Don't dare insult the chef. Sit. Eat. I've got twenty minutes."

Dharma chewed and rolled her eyes in delight. "Delish! Did you really mean what you said before? I can still come visit after school starts?"

"Flights are barely more than a hundred dollars. Fly here Friday, fly back Sunday." Should've done that lives ago, but before, he never had the time; he still didn't, but decided he must make the time. Otherwise, life wasn't sustainable.

"Since when do you bake?"

"Life experience. Save some room. The cinnamon twists will be done in five. Tell me again, why are pirates better than ninjas?"

Interrupted from cutting her tart, Dharma slammed her fork down. "Dad, everyone knows ninjas are the best. Oh sure, pirates are great at frontal assault, but ninja's . . . They're subtle. They can topple a dynasty with a single blow."

#

Kartar took a break from his workstation and looked around. Guy, the DB developer who joined them from Donny's team had gelled well with the others. He and Rockstar pair programed with two keyboards plugged into one computer, the display mirrored so they could collaborate as seamlessly as possible. Prince went over something with LG and Theckla. Last week, they had gotten ahold of an Allen wrench and took down most of the cubicle walls, making one big "pod" and reducing email overuse. The Allen wrench made the rounds: Donny's team Ka–ching, and Noah's team, now called 'Agent Smith' (because now every team built architecture as well as features), converted to pods with the PMs sitting alongside their team members.

Kartar studied a freestanding whiteboard, upon which sat the Sprint's task board. They'd settled on columns Planned, In Progress, Verify, and Accepted. Guy and Rockstar were still In Progress on Single Wheel Slot's animation. Yesterday, Rockstar and Prince had pair programmed on the 'Bling Bling Bling!' story, named after the noise traditional slot machines make when you win. That story card was now in the Verify column. Across the pod, Prince, LG, and Theckla huddled at Prince's workstation from which came a clang, clang,

clang, with more sounds and flashing colors. They began discussing animation and strobe effects when Rockstar suddenly left his pairing session and walked over.

"Hold on a patch! We already thought about that! The handheld's screen resolution may not be good enough for that level of detail."

Theckla nodded. "OK. We'll work with this until we get the hardware to do some look–n–feel."

Kartar hid a smile behind a book of stickies. Getting teams and PMs in one area had really sped up decision making. Once they were all in a small location, collaboration became as effortless as breathing.

He shook his head, thinking about how bad things had gotten under the old way of working. Somewhere along the river ride of Waterfall, meetings had become synonymous with collaboration. This made collaboration something measurable, incited by management via calendar events. Now, collaboration was a matter of nature, invisible unless you were watching for it. Direct management of the project was as unnecessary and heavy–handed as having a manager coordinate the social calendar between friends. Communication had become dynamic. And, Kartar admitted to himself, scary. As he no longer organized "collaboration" in the form of meetings, he no longer knew every decision that was made, and had no 'paper trail' of meeting events.

He looked at the class diagrams on the whiteboard, then looked around the pod. Shouldn't feel that way, he decided. Every day, collaboration happened before his eyes.

He knocked loudly on the task board. "Standup!"

LG, Theckla, and Prince continued to talk as they walked to the task board. Rockstar and Guy kept working, Rockstar's finger pointing at something on Guy's screen and Guy typing furiously.

Theckla formed a cone with her hands and yelled, "Guys! Guys!"

Rockstar and Guy were so focused, they jumped at the interruption.

Rockstar said, "Sorry lads, we were adding momentum to the wheel spin."

Kartar stayed silent as everyone collected around the board, even stepping to the side to avoid appearing as the meeting leader. He counted slowly to ten. Still only silence.

"So nobody did anything?" he quipped.

"Prince and I finished the Bling Bling Bling! story," Rockstar said, "We had to adjust the detail on some images due to screen resolution."

"Yes," Theckla said. "It's OK for now."

"And what is it now?" blurted Kartar. He still desperately wanted to hear details so he could validate or make a decision, even though he knew it wasn't his place to do so in Agile.

Theckla said, "It looks flat."

"I'll give you a demo after standup," said Prince.

Theckla said, "I'd like a 3D effect. You know, light shining from top left, but we'll accept the story since we don't know if the hardware can support it."

LG's eyes narrowed but she didn't say anything. Theckla was the Product Owner for Wow, so LG'd have to wait for Daily Scrum to finish working out her concerns.

Kartar said, "Why not—erumph—," clamping lips shut and shaking his head for them to continue. It was easy to sympathize with LG; he wanted to push for the best and shiniest too. In past lives, he or LG or Theckla would talk 90% of the time in meetings, the developers' eyes glazing over while the three argued over how to best use development resources. Now, he practiced listening, trusting those doing the work to make good decisions. A kind of trust that was incredibly damn hard to give because it was so different—the opposite, really—of what he'd done in the past. But if any project needed to be different, this was it.

Kartar silently wrote 'video specs?' on a sticky note and stuck it on the task board on the area labeled: impediments. LG mouthed, "Thank you."

Theckla moved the sticky labeled 'Bling Bling Bling!' to the 'Accepted' column.

Kartar said, "Good work and congratulations to Prince and Rockstar on finishing that story." The two looked embarrassed but proud as everyone clapped or patted them on the back. "And the way Guy is pairing on UI stories, he'll soon be developing widgets."

Prince turned to Rockstar and Guy and said, "Now I've got nothing to do until you guys finish, then I can start Pay Out."

"Why can't you start now?" Guy asked.

"Because your code will call mine. . . . It'll be easier to do it afterwards."

Rockstar frowned and said, "Just build what you need —"

"And do test driven development so we have unit tests," Guy finished.

"Right," said Rockstar. "And whomever finishes last deals with the merge conflicts." Rockstar mimed throwing a gauntlet onto the floor.

"You're on!" said Prince, smiling.

The end of fifteen minutes neared. Kartar said, "Any impediments to list?"

Prince squinted one eye, looking sideways at Rockstar and Guy. "Well, with Kong busy being Captain UI on Ka–ching, I don't have a pairing partner."

Rockstar pointed at Kartar. "What about Elvis? I bet

he knows how to sling some code."

Kartar blushed. "Well, it's been a long time. And I'm more of a C++ guy."

Prince patted Kartar on the back. "Don't worry. I'll keep you from coding us into a ditch."

"Impediment solved. Good work Scrum Master," Theckla said.

So this is it, Kartar thought while following Prince back to his workstation. Speak three sentences at a fifteen minute meeting, write down an impediment, and became the key to resolving a second impediment by directive from the team. Could this be the 'servant leadership' J'd mentioned? Get the team to tell you what they need, and don't disappoint them. Otherwise, you're just another manager.

The teams continued this way for weeks. . . .

#

After work one night, Kartar found a leaf with writing on it tucked beneath one of his car's wiper blades. He slid it from the window, assuming someone had found one of his and stuck it there. As he got behind the wheel, he gave it a glance:

Your questions about smoothly transitioning from Waterfall to Agile were good. From what you've written, it sounds like things are proceeding well. For a dynamic industry such as IT, we're inexperienced at changing our software lifecycle because we've never done anything beyond tweak our existing doctrine of Waterfall, which was developed in the 1950s. What you've done is a big change. There will be push back from those who don't like the change, and they will attack what you're doing, just as your antibodies would of a foreign object. Better to get the organizational antibodies on your side rather than fight them.

With three brand new Scrum teams, you're going to have three information silos (this is good and bad). Adding a process called Scrum of Scrums would give those teams an opportunity to increase cross–team learning. Here are a few links on how to get started.

...

Be courageous, be flexible, be Agile,
J

Angry, Kartar crumpled the leaf and tossed it out the window. It answered none of his questions. He was being played. J'd finally come out of hiding, only to write random advice on a leaf and leave it to be found.

He backed out of the parking space but quickly stopped the car, having a sudden change of heart—how could J even know him as they have yet to meet during this lifetime? In fact, it was two lifetimes ago when they'd met in De'Arte's bar. Wasn't this leaf proof that someone other than himself knew about his previous lives? And to tell the truth, that 'Scrum of Scrums' sounded interesting.

He got out and stretched down to get the leaf. A breeze tumbled it to a few parking spots away. He walked toward it, and a wind sent it tumbling again. Cursing, he pursued it like a ball in a soccer match until finally pinning it in place with his foot. Breathing heavily, he sat in his car and read it again, then stared through the windshield, lost in thought.

#

After getting a Venetian Raspberry latte, Kartar found a table to stand at in the corner. On a napkin, he wrote the following:

30 minute time box
Each talk on these points:
What's holding the team back?
What new discovery or breakthrough was made?
What support does my team need from the organization or another team?

Donny and Noah arrived as he was writing, and gave coffee orders to the barista.

Donny bumped between Kartar and Noah, a big grin on his face, his sunglasses perched on his forehead as always. "I have to tell you guys," he cocked his head and looked Kartar in the eye "regardless of whether or not we actually keep to this schedule, it's been exciting having feature teams. You know, DBAs are a quiet and regulated crowd . . . like they're all on Valium. Switch things up so you have two developers and two DBA's? You get exciting discussion. If standup starts going long or people get too detailed, Kong beats his chest like a gorilla and says, 'take it offline.' "

Kartar nodded. "Guy's getting used to us. He looked pretty panicked the first two weeks, when the devs kept telling him they didn't already know what entity models they'd need and would tell him as they discovered them."

Noah grinned. "I saw Kartar pair programming with Prince. So you enjoyed that?"

Kartar brushed back his pompadour. "I'll say this about Pairing. That session made understanding impediments and technical challenges ultra–clear. Even sitting with the team has helped. I don't need to give anyone the third degree anymore because I just know. And yes, it's nice being a direct contributor."

"So I know what you mean," Noah said. "When I worked on architecture teams for other projects, although we got a lot of cool technical work, we never directly implemented features. That made it difficult to communicate with business about our contribution. With our team directly building features for operations, both ops and business are excited. There isn't any question about how we contribute. And—"

Noah tidied a loose hair into his ponytail while he paused. "So the idea about emergent architecture has forced me and the team to think differently. We only build what's necessary for the features we're delivering in the current Sprint, and with you guys doing the same, no one is waiting for someone else to build what's needed. I'm still concerned about trying to enhance something built by a different team and developer. How's that going to work?"

"Unit Tests man," said Donny. "No single person owns the code. Everyone adjusting each other's code would be bedlam, you're right about that. Except the unit tests guard functionality far better than any documentation, or even the author for that matter."

Noah nodded. "True. That makes me feel better. And Donny, our new DBA team member is using a migration–driven development workflow for migrating schema and data to new models—so thank you. The script is part of our 'source code and build' process. She'll demo it to you and your team so you can drive DB changes too. I've tossed the design docs entirely. The team consistently came up with better solutions for the problems at hand.

"So I think all this is rooted in what Benjamin Franklin said about, 'necessity being the mother of invention.' That's how we're doing it—building only what's demonstratively necessary for the Sprint."

Noah paused, a pained expression emerging.

"But," Kartar prompted.

"But we need something more." Again, Noah pulled back his already–organized hair and fiddled with the scrunchie.

"Integration," said Kartar.

"Exactly!" Noah and Donny said together.

Noah shook his head. "Sprint end is coming up—"

"And the Sprint Demo," said Donny, jabbing finger against the coffee table. "How are we going to have your 'working software' demo–able?"

Kartar nodded. "And we should spend no more than an hour preparing."

Donny's stomach gurgled; the sound made the three smile.

"Exactly!" said Noah. "So how are we going to do this?"

Kartar nodded. "Sounds like we need to talk with our teams."

Noah shook his head. "You mean we're going to come up with a plan first."

"No he does not!" Donny belled hard against the table and leaned aggressively into Kartar's personal space. Kartar's drink tipped precariously, but Noah steadied it. Donny jabbed a finger into Kartar's chest. "You're saying you don't know? I don't believe this! Of all the—"

Kartar said, "Hold on! Remember, the team owns the process. We get them to tell us what they need, and we support their decision. We simply ask them what must be done to demo their features to DeLucca."

Noah shook his head. "So you really want to add that fuel to this burning house? Now?"

"Burning house?" Kartar said. "What burning house? You both just said things were OK—"

Noah nodded to Kartar's point. "So maybe we should just have LG be a proxy for DeLucca. DeLucca's a Vice President!"

Donny nodded. "Yeah, I'm with him. A Vice President in that meeting is a little like bringing a battleship when you only need a frigate."

Kartar said, "We need the team to know this potentially shippable software must be of shippable quality, as if a player would use it. And DeLucca is really who we're building this for."

"I see." Donny nodded. "DeLucca trying out Winner in the demo would be even scarier to the teams." He snapped fingers together. "Ah ha! You really are some kinda evil Elvis. I get your angle! We scare the crap out of 'em to get quality."

Noah wagged his head side to side. "It certainly puts the fear of failure in them. However, I don't know how Theckla has been working it out with you guys, but I can tell you that LG is sometimes guessing at what to do for our Play 'n Rewards story."

Kartar pushed back his pompadour with a finger then swung the digit forward to point it at Noah. "Yes! That's the other reason we need DeLucca. Of course LG is unclear what DeLucca wants. I know DeLucca is unsure what he wants. We're developing something brand new. He needs to see if we are close to hitting the target, or . . . he needs to see something that inspires a new idea, a better idea. We need to keep the customer in the center of development, and DeLucca's the one."

Donny nodded. "Yeah, he's the one that'll cause heads to roll."

Noah nodded, pinching his lips together while in thought. "OK. So . . . so we are doing something collaborative. So it's creative and we'll influence each other. So DeLucca will give us the clearest picture of what the target is. Anything less would be working through a middleman." Noah kept nodding as the ideas took hold. "We want that pressure. And we need to frequently integrate our work to know when features stop operating."

Kartar held his coffee out to toast Noah. "Exactly! I expect our teams will want to start doing integration tests. I've been waiting for them to discover we need better and more frequent integration than we had during this Sprint."

Noah nodded. "Yeah, it's our first 'practice' release"

Donny slapped hands together. "And we're seeing before our very eyes the challenges in operating this fast."

Kartar nodded. "And we'll get better next Sprint. We'll talk about our troubles during the Sprint Retrospective, and adjust our plans. And the three of us should to communicate with each other about the solutions our teams come up with."

"I see," said Noah. "Because they're the ones doing the work."

Donny nodded. "You know, this is sounding more and more like how the University of Miami football program operated. My freshman and sophomore years were failures. We hardly won a game until my junior year, when we got a new head coach. He kept saying, 'Look guys, I can't do all the thinking for you. You guys are on the field seeing what you're seeing. You need to tell me what you need.' "

"How did that go?" asked Noah.

"It was a turnaround season. Got a division championship! But the next season, we won the big one." He held up his ring.

Noah said, "Well, in three Sprints, we have a serious game to win."

They all nodded and Kartar pondered how little Donny and Noah understood the gravity of the situation. It was dead serious.

Donny said, "How about we start your 'Scrum of Scrums' meeting?"

Kartar flipped over his napkin. "Our thirty minute time–box has expired. This was our meeting agenda."

Noah laughed. "Nice! And it's exactly what we did. When do we do this again?"

"We meet as needed to bubble up and solve problems too big for one team. We shouldn't need to wait until a set event occurs. But since we've got Sprint One's demo coming up, and we're going to get input back from our teams about how to resolve integration testing, so let's say the day after tomorrow?"

Donny and Noah nodded.

For the second time, Noah gave Kartar a warm pat on the shoulder. Kartar watched them leave, thinking about the past life when Noah wanted to game the Gantt. Then, just as he had now, Noah seemed to exhibit genuine friendship. But the smell of green tea lotion lingered along with memories of Noah expanding head count or overreaching into UI architecture. What was certain was that Noah would try something.

When Noah made his move, he'd be ready.

#

The team sat around a conference room table. Theckla looked at her watch for the tenth time, then at Kartar. "He's fifteen minutes late."

Rockstar looked at each person sitting around the table in the eye and said, "We need a brave lad to go get him. Any volunteers? No? Then I volunteer Guy. He's the 'new' guy on the team."

Prince raised his hand, "Seconded!"

Guy's eyes opened big. "But he's vice president!"

Kartar looked at Guy. "Hmm . . . Not a bad—"

The door opened. "Oh thank Sparta!" said Guy. But his face fell when it was LG who entered.

"Where's DeLucca?" asked Kartar.

"Sorry I'm late. He was on the phone when I passed

his door."

Kartar made a face while pulling out his cell phone and dialing DeLucca's office. The room quieted enough to hear the AC rushing through a vent; everyone was still. And listening.

DeLucca answered. "Sorry, I've got the money on the other line now."

"We're holding up the meeting for you in High Roller," said Kartar.

"Let's reschedule for tomorrow."

"Tomorrow, we start Sprint Two. Today, you also have Ka–ching and Agent Smith's demos. You don't want to delay all three teams. That would eat up a day of development, slowing all of us down."

"Three hours of meetings! In one day! You're killing me."

Kartar held phone to ear while walking to the meeting room door. Somehow, the room seemed larger and took more steps to cross it than it should have. Donny and Noah's team filed in as he stepped out and closed the door. The hallway suddenly darkened as if the sunlight had dimmed, like a partial eclipse.

Kartar spoke into his phone. "You promised to collaborate so this project would be successful."

"Well, I don't recall promising to meet for three hours —"

"We've had this meeting on the calendar for two weeks. We need you to see our work. Six hours a month isn't asking much."

"Be reasonable! They're waiting on the other line."

"Then tell them you've got a commitment you must attend to. They're always demanding their commitments be met, so they'll understand. This isn't a typical corporate meeting. We're demonstrating games your players will be spending money on. You're going to be seeing the first draft of what we'll be releasing in eight weeks."

He waited, sensing DeLucca's indecision. "This is THE meeting. This is where you'll see the pure unadulterated truth of how the money is being spent."

DeLucca stayed silent, so Kartar added, "We can't be successful without you. And those people on the phone require success."

"I'll see what I can do," said DeLucca.

Kartar returned to the meeting and his seat, and everyone silently tried to read his face.

"Keep the projector warmed up. He'll be right down."

DeLucca entered as Prince showed another variation of Bat Versus Bunny, a shadow puppet drama.

"Sorry I'm late," he said, shaking rolled cuffs loose and buttoning them back at his wrists with silver cuff links. "Let's see what you've got."

The team introduced the Sprint stories they'd worked on, Spin, Lose, and, Bling–Bling–Bling! Kartar watched the boss carefully, assessing every facial twitch and blink. When Prince or Rockstar made quips, DeLucca took them in stride and added his own as the devs demonstrated the slot machine through roleplaying player archetypes.

DeLucca applauded the team's work at the end. "You're setting the bar high for the next two teams."

Prince said, "You mean we're going to win at Scrum?"

"That depends on you getting this delivered," said DeLucca. His tone became serious. "Will we have hardware for the next Sprint?"

"Yes," said Theckla. "We'll have the first generation ready, which we're expecting in quantities of five hundred for our rollout. The first shipment is in transit."

DeLucca clapped his hands. "Superb! So when do I see our Gantt chart?"

Kartar shook his head. "There is no Gantt because we're measuring progress with something more valuable —the number of fully tested and defect–free features."

DeLucca's face clouded. "Well, these auditors are going to want it. The stakeholders got upset when I told them we were doing something different."

Donny and Noah looked at Kartar.

DeLucca shook his head. "Don't worry about it. I backed you up. But auditors will be checking on things."

Noah's eyes rolled. Donny looked worried and said, "We can put something together if—"

Kartar shook his head. "Let's not add more reporting on top of what we're already doing. We'll integrate the auditors into Scrum reporting mechanisms: task boards, Sprint Burndowns, Release Burnups, and Sprint Demo. We already require those activities so let's not add overhead to our execution."

DeLucca shook his head. "That's going to cause trouble. They've got their own way of doing things. Send the Gantt to me later."

While Kartar's face reddened, DeLucca slapped his hands together. "Let's see what Ka–ching and Agent Smith's got cooking!"

SUSTAINABLE PACE

With Sprint One behind them, work became rhythmic. Every fifteen–minute Daily Scrum, Kartar listened to his team and posted his commitments to solve impediments on the task board alongside the team's work. Whenever DeLucca or LG emailed questions about requirements, Kartar invited them to the next Daily Scrum so they could discuss them immediately afterward. When DeLucca was there, it was hard to keep silent because he felt compelled to take responsibility for answering his questions rather than just letting the team handle them. With lips mashed together, he kept himself from jumping in, because as Donny had said, 'software development was a team's game, not the coach's.'

With the cubicle walls down, individual team members were no longer separated. The walls that remained were the borders to other teams and each team used a wall to post their Sprint Backlog, in front of which they'd hold their Daily Scrum and update the board's status. The three team 'pods' were bound by the building's walls. At the center of one wall, Noah had mounted a forty–five inch flat screen that loomed over the pods, because, as he was fond of saying, "You shouldn't have to look into the status of the build, the build status should be looking into you." And look into them it did. For the next four days, the build monitor showed the team's failing integration tests with simple red danger colors, even making rude noises for follow–on builds that failed to improve the status. When nothing improved for a week, Theckla added more pressure. After each day of failure, she brought to work a new part of a 'hangman' created with her 3D printer. Day by day, a piece was added: a noose with rope, then a head made of white plastic (which Prince said looked like an Indian Elvis). After arms and shoulders were added, the figurine was given a purple shirt, then one leg ending with a Birkenstock–clad foot, and then a guitar.

"So we're all complicit," said Noah looking down at his sandals. "We keep finding other things to do."

Day by day, everyone got more and more stressed until finally, after a UM championship ring was added, Prince, Kong, and Noah cleared their day of other concerns and solved the issues preventing automated deployment and data setup. The build monitor finally showed green, saving the hangman one leg short of doom.

Kartar's inbox received few emails. If something was important, you'd simply turn around and talk to someone. If they were busy pair programming, maybe you'd leave a sticky on the task board so the question didn't get lost. Communication amongst the teams became face–to–face conversations.

Communication from the business changed as well. Theckla moved into Wow's pod. LG, however, kept her windowed office near DeLucca's. Not everyone could change so easily.

During Sprint Two, Kartar was at his desk when Theckla arrived with a bunch of freezer paper and recruited Donny to help hang it on the wall. The room quieted as some developers stopped to see what was up.

Theckla said to Donny, "Why shouldn't the rest of us use brainstorms, stickies, and task boards like the development team?"

Theckla left and the room built into a buzz of activity. Noah's team started Daily Scrum. Wow's pair programming, which never really stopped, rose in intensity. Donny's team congratulated him on his 'talent' of hanging blank tapestry.

Theckla returned with a deck of sticky notes and LG, who carried an armful of documents. LG read each requirement aloud as Theckla wrote the highlights on stickies and stuck them on the wall. How turning something virtual into something physical with such a simple step could change things so radically, Kartar would have never have guessed. And it all happened in one day.

While he was on the phone with the shipping company, checking on their hardware, LG and Theckla's discussion at the wall had gone from cautious to heated. Noah tapped Kartar on the shoulder.

"You'd better go talk to them."

Donny was already there, trying to get a word in edgewise, but the situation wasn't improving. Theckla's face was the same shade of red as her glasses, and LG frowned and white knuckled her pen like she prepared to to skewer something.

On the wall behind them, the items prioritized for the first release were in 'user story' format. The next release's plan was detailed by one–line descriptions called 'epics,' one per sticky.

Kartar said to Noah, "Call DeLucca and tell him he's missing an important requirements meeting."

"You do it," Noah said but Kartar gestured at his earwig indicating he was on a call.

"Fine," Noah said. "I'll call the old man."

Everyone half–listened to the fight, but work didn't stop.

DeLucca walked in while LG lobbied Donny for support: "We need to lock things down for the next four releases."

Theckla stood her ground. "Let's not mask uncertainty behind decisions that will only need changing later."

DeLucca watched the two until the white paper covered with sticky notes stole his attention. He stepped past, letting them continue arguing.

After studying the wall he said, "Can we move this epic into Sprint Three?"

The analysts turned to see what he had in hand. LG snatched the sticky to wave it at Thekla. "See? If we had all the details written down, we could immediately answer his question. Sticky notes won't work."

"No big deal," Theckla said. "We have until Sprint Three planning to get the analysis done."

DeLucca snatched it back from LG, the look on his face saying everything for him, and stuck it cockeyed among the column of stickies for Sprint Three. "I see what's happening here. Strategic planning for the future, and detailed planning for the next Sprint and a half. Good idea! Until I hold the Winner in my hand and experience what it's like, we're mostly guessing."

From that day onward, requirements meetings came out of the 'back room' and into the team area where developers or PMs could join at any moment. As a side effect, emails and phone calls about requirements became face–to–face meetings because the project's backlog was tracked on a physical wall.

The tools of the work influenced behavior.

Kartar left for home early so he and Dharma could walk together before dark. Today, a three–inch roadrunner scurried across their path and they followed it to the shadows of the development's water fountain.

"Let's catch it," said Kartar, and together they crawled forward on their hands and knees. Dirt got on his chinos and Dharma kept laughing.

"What?" He turned and looked at his daughter, smiling at the giant grin on her face.

"Do you remember how you used to give me rides like you were a horse?" Her laughter poured out in a clarity that competed with the gurgling water, until she ended in a snort. Embarrassed, she tried to distract him by walking on her knees, closing in on the animal.

When her shadow fell over it, it realized it was trapped between her and the fountain's foundation, so it turned and charged. She squealed and fell back on the ground as it ran toward her. It used her leg as a ramp, leaped past her head, and ran away.

She sat up and watched it go, a hand covering her heart. "Oh, I thought I was a goner." She flopped onto her back, laughing. Kartar did the same, wrapping an arm around her.

"Dad," Dharma said staring into the blue Nevada sky. "This has been the best summer of my life. I wish I could see you more than just weekends. I wish school didn't start next week."

#

DeLucca was no help when it came to Lovers. After pouring two drinks of twenty–year–old Scotch, he said, "Find a way to make them happy. Otherwise things'll go to hell."

Recalling what J said about getting the 'antibodies' on his side, Kartar prepped with Donny and Noah. They set up the meeting in the executive board room, usually reserved for Casino VPs: minibar with alcoholic and non–alcoholic drinks, organic snacks catered to the room, and coffee delivered from SciFi Coffee.

As they entered the meeting, Kartar's voice died upon seeing Sis and Lex waiting at one end of the long mahogany table. The Winner PMs crowded together at the opposite end, crammed elbow to elbow. Sis sat upright, white leather jacket—collarless or "Indian style"—unbuttoned over a white blouse, hair pulled back into a severe bun, her blue eyes sweeping across them as they filed in. Lex wore a black, one–piece Dior dress with big lapels cut like a bathrobe, posture slouched like a laborer, head propped on fist to stare out the window overlooking Casino parking. Elegant and put–upon, like her smoking break had been rudely interrupted.

The PMs sat as one, silent. On Kartar's right, Noah simply stared at the two women, studying them it seemed. To his left, Donny shyly glanced at Sis then at the table, and then back to her again. The group remained still and quiet, unsure as to who should start. Sis leaned forward, her collar showing part of the designer label, surely "Laraette" or something from Neiman Marcus. Killers were paid better than IT managers.

Kartar started before she could speak. "Well." He looked at the space between the Lovers rather than directly at either. "Let's start by going through our five levels of planning."

He talked through their Vision statement and Donny helped fill in the details whenever he slowed. Sis watched them talk, her eyes never leaving the face of the man speaking. Lex occasionally glanced their way, then returned to gazing out the window, petulant, like the whole thing was beneath her. Kartar moved on to their four box roadmap which outlined what major features would be in the four releases they planned to do within the year.

Sis half stood, startling Lex who, like there was a sudden danger, crouched low behind the table. Kartar thanked the gods she didn't draw her gun.

"Wait!" Sis said. "Four releases!?"

Kartar then noticed Noah was doing the same as Lex, crouched, watching her, his right hand worrying at his pantleg.

"Yes," said Kartar, giving an odd look to Noah and Lex, who both stood slowly. "Drop something?" he asked Lex who sat down, ignoring him. "It's an incremental delivery model. We are going to satisfy our customers through early and continuous delivery of valuable software—"

Lex wrote in the notebook before her: 'Kartar' followed by a slash.

Kartar's throat closed. The heat, the desert, his car tumbling off the freeway while the sky through his windshield swapped places with desert sand. Knee throbbing. Sis leaning above him while the Strip's river of headlights shimmered below. Thousands of people passing beneath while he bled out on the monorail track. The explosion in his garage. They always came for him. They always got him. Always he was dying.

Noah had been speaking for a while, Kartar realized. Each time Sis said, "Excuse me," Noah interrupted back, always saying "So I'm getting to the point," and continuing on, covering how they planned four releases instead of one big release to get early market feedback, reduce project risk, and start earning revenue more quickly.

Sis listened, jaw hanging open at the affront to her management sensibilities. Although the meeting had been setup for her, it was clear she didn't hold the floor.

Lex scanned the room through narrowed eyes, her hand nestled in her bag, the muscle connecting elbow to wrist tensing whenever someone's hands dropped beneath the table. The more Sis got upset, the more intense Lex's attentions. She no longer gazed out the window, bored. Rather, she seemed keenly focused, as if, Kartar imagined, mentally administering gun katas to prepare the most effective way to lay waste to her annoyances.

Noah kept speaking, ignoring the room's negative tone. He explained how their Agile strategy avoided the faults of a "big bang" release by delivering frequently. Donny nodded and added a few words here and there, a charming smile on the big man's face. He rolled his chair closer to Sis, often stretching his hand across the table, toward her, gesturing emphatically as he made his points.

Kartar grabbed the back of Donny's chair and returned him to his place. He ignored the 'what gives?' look Noah and Donny gave him. If only they knew, he thought. If only they knew these two women held their lives in their palms. No matter what happened now, using Agile had transcended from being his whim to everyone's intention. With J's manifesto as a guiding light, they supported each other in ways that actually contributed to delivering the project.

Donny shook his head at Kartar then pushed himself out of his chair, went to the whiteboard and talked through the third level of planning, the Release Plan.

"It's a work versus time chart to help us predict when we'll finish the first box in the road map. The Y axis is the level of effort for all the requirements for the release. The X axis is the number of Sprints before release. As each Sprint completes, the actual progress is marked on the chart. We use a linear regression to predict the number of Sprints needed to deliver all the requirements. You see, it allows for more or fewer requirements to be delivered by a fixed release date."

Donny turned to Sis who hadn't spoken for twenty minutes. "Now Sis, you're going to appreciate the fact that, unlike a complex Gantt filled with subjective results on percentage of 'done,' this simple chart allows us to see how the project is progressing months in advance so we can adjust accordingly. We only 'burn up' completed work—work that has been QAed and is shippable."

She rocked her head side–to–side, rubbing her neck to release stress.

Noah demonstrated the fourth level of planning, the Sprint Plan, and summarized what his team had accomplished when a Lover finally spoke.

"Em. All this is so grand," said Lex. Emphasizing how she really felt, she continued to speaking while staring out the window. "When do we get to the chart?"

"Chart?" asked Noah.

"Yeah. Ye' know." Lex waved her hand. "That . . . chart."

Sis nodded. "The Gantt chart. It's the standard for assessing project health. Like breathing, it's something everyone does—"

"And wants te' continue doing," finished Lex.

Donny and Noah glanced nervously at Kartar, who pulled a document from his papers. "Here. It's derived from the road map so it doesn't add any additional information." He handed it to Donny, who used his chair to roll to Lex, who handed it to Sis. Donny stayed nearby until Lex shot him a look that sent him rolling quickly back.

"Mr. Patel," Sis said. "This can't be correct. Although you've got three parallel streams for the three teams, you have nearly no dependencies."

Donny smiled at Sis and ignored Lex's cold stare. "We've organized ourselves to eliminate dependencies. This is a road map level Gantt. It has a prediction to when the entire four releases are finished and—"

"How can you do any work with this kind of Gantt? How can you build something as complicated as a new product and not have dependencies? And QA should be dependent on all of this. How—"

Noah said, "We are feature teams. Each of our developers and QA professionals work on implementing entire features and work with the BAs—"

"And DeLucca, and all the VPs," Kartar added.

Noah nodded. "Yes. So . . . so we have conversations about complete features, drastically reducing problems caused by dependencies that normally fragment development, requirement communication, and feature testing. In fact . . ."

Noah stood and wrote 'effective' on the whiteboard. "We could be even more effective if we knew more about the stakeholders. At the end of every Sprint, we have a Sprint Demo where we play Winner's games. We want to invite them in so they can see how the project is progressing with their own eyes, and try the product they're funding with their own hands."

Kartar glanced at Noah, wondering when he'd decided to push for more face–to–face communication and collaboration. Last they talked, Noah had asked for names regarding the project funders, but DeLucca wouldn't say.

"Yes," Kartar said. "If they actually try out the Winner, they'll have a more accurate picture than any Gantt or—"

Lex shook her head. "Ye' living fantasy. Ye' can't expect the stakeholders to come and meet at ye' beck and call."

Before Kartar could respond, Noah replied, "So if they're so busy they can't be bothered to learn accurate results for the millions they're spending, why not help us make the reporting lightweight? Or put us in contact with someone we can work with so we can determine what reporting is useful, rather than just relying on templates."

Lex watched Sis sit quietly, stabbing pen into paper. Lex scribbled something in her notebook. Donny tried to peek, but she covered it and glared.

Kartar shrugged. "Regardless of the changes in reporting, we'll have our first release in a few weeks and they'll see results on the casino floor."

Noah nodded. "True. But better to start building a relationship with them as soon as possible."

Lex added another note, a quick pen stroke. She looked at Sis. Their eyes connected. Lex's face and alabaster skin seemed frozen in an icy frown, the eyebrows rigid, only the pen quivering in hand giving off any indication she was functional. Sis raised hand to mouth and bit a knuckle hard enough that Donny gasped.

Lex said, "Don't gnaw love. Ye' know what that does to me." She looked at the PMs and shook her head. "Ye' forgetting somethin' important. We're in charge. Our process. Our rules. Let's see yer . . ."

"Work Breakdown Structure," finished Sis.

Noah stood, and like someone who would declare 'Eureka!' in another context, exclaimed "WDIWT!"

Donny and Kartar looked at each other, alarmed, because nothing good ever happened when Noah reached this point.

"Wood wit?" asked Lex, looking at Sis who shook her head too.

"Excuse me, nature calls," Noah declared, and strode out.

Kartar looked askance at the closing door, then came

to Donny's aid in explaining how they weren't using a WBS since work wasn't assigned until the Sprint Planning, and how they used the Velocity model in lieu of traditional capacity planning.

Like Sis was in a slow–motion video, her eyes widened every minute Donny spoke, and her hands, frame by frame, curled tighter and tighter into white fists. Lex monitored her partner's increasing agitation, flicking her eyes between Sis and the men in ever quickening shifts.

Sis interrupted. "I'm sorry Mr. Biglow, but what I'm hearing is that you aren't managing your resources."

"But people aren't resources, they're people," stressed Donny. He spoke faster as Sis got more unsettled: shifting, squinting, wincing, sometimes biting her lip until maybe there was danger she'd actually bite through. Her agitation seemed to infect Donny, who fidgeting likewise as he rambled on, until finally, he interrupted himself. "—Agile is a really different process." He looked at Kartar for help.

Lex's notebook listed each of their names on a different row followed by a series of lines. She's counting the number of responses, Kartar realized. She's trying to decide who to blame. The PMs were nearly even.

"With Velocity," Donny said. "We use each team's most recent results to plan for the upcoming Sprint. This is much more accurate than a WBS and Perfect Planning."

Following some invisible cue, each Lover removed her bag from the table and set it on her lap.

Kartar's ears rang as if guns were already discharging. They're going to absolutely shoot us in several painful ways, he said to himself. Donny must've heard, because he gave Kartar a 'say what?' look.

Sis shook her head and spoke, voice quavering. "What

you have done is so far out of process, I don't know where to begin."

Donny's face turned red. Before he could speak, Lex hissed, "Stop. Ye' don't get to talk."

Sis, posture ramrod straight, blond hair shinning in the sun, hands folded on the table in front of her, continued. "This is entirely out of process. No. That's too kind. There is no process. You're not following any established protocol for professional software delivery."

Kartar didn't bother preparing a response beyond hitting the floor at any sudden move.

Donny shook his head. "But don't you see? This is better. Come to our Sprint Demo and you'll see what I mean. You don't need those reports—"

Lex added another tick after Donny's name, and Kartar felt alternating waves of guilt and relief that Donny had the most lines.

Sis raised a hand to silence him. "We require those documents. Our stakeholders demand we give them those documents. We use them to do risk analysis. There are tons of activities supported by those documents."

While Sis lectured, a grin warmed at Lex's mouth, growing to an open–mouthed smile as she seemed to contemplate something immensely enjoyable.

"And," Sis continued, "the stakeholders have no interest in early releases with partial functionality. They care about the whole thing being finished on time. You're adding more overhead and risk by doing four releases instead of just one." She laughed and turned to Lex. "I mean, who does that? Use four releases to get done what should only require one?"

She glowered at Kartar. "You're a registered PMI Professional. You know better!"

Lex added a tick to his name. Tied again with Donny.

Kartar imagined the guns would come out any second.

If it happened now, he couldn't defend himself. So he pushed for reason.

"You're a high priestess of the PMI. A professional of your level should be adaptable and open minded. There's more to software delivery than Waterfall. If there ever was a project that needed to respond to change over following a plan, it's this one!"

Her chair shot back as she sprung to her feet, knuckles on the table, opening her mouth to say something that no one heard because a fire alarm started to ring.

Donny and Kartar used the opportunity to hustle out and ran down the hallway like the Prada–toting devils were right behind.

"What are we going to do?" Donny yelled over the racket, taking two stairs with each stride.

"We give them a WBS."

"How?"

"Makeup some fiction that matches today's reality."

At a landing, Donny paused to glance at him.

Kartar rolled his eyes. "Come on! That's what we used to do. Only this time, we won't spend so much time believing the B.S.."

Noah found them in the parking lot. "Pretty inconvenient timing for a fire drill, huh?"

"Thank the gods!" said Kartar. "I didn't see it on the calendar."

Noah grinned. "It was called in at the last minute."

Donny whistled.

"Smart!" said Kartar. "That way the alarm lever doesn't smell like sencha."

"What?" Noah shook his head, confused. Which, in a way, made sense since Noah hadn't started listening in on Kartar's meetings until months later in the project. So far this time around, they hadn't argued like they had in past lives. But this fire alarm stunt .... Could the man he suspected of throwing him under the bus really be an ally?

"Nothing," said Kartar.

"Come on," Noah said, "Let's do a 'Scrum of Scrums' while we're out here. So ... we've all got a major impediment." He led them to the far side of the parking garage as he talked. "It would appear they're unwilling to adjust reporting to fit our new way of working, and I don't think any of us are willing to switch back to the old way just to make the reports look pretty."

Kartar whistled, shaking his head in admiration. It had finally happened! Developers now did their best on the Sprint Backlog. The management team made decisions to serve the team and make the project stronger, rather than to look good in reports. Communication had morphed from trading emails to face–to–face conversations that quickly exposed knowledge and solutions. The business collaborated with the teams daily. Transparency had increased. It was no longer just his project, nor DeLucca's, nor LG's, nor . . . . They all were committed to delivering software. Finally! Organized and aligned to a single goal, just as the Lovers were. Would it be enough to overcome murder?

Donny shook his head. "They didn't listen to a word we said. I don't know about you two, but I feel attacked. It's like something, or someone, within the casino doesn't want this change and . . ."

Kartar nodded. "They attacked us like some kind of antibody. If they don't understand what you're doing, they kill you."

"WDIWT?" Noah said. "Lovers are just enforcement. Something is guiding them. What do you know about who's funding the project?"

Kartar shook his head. "DeLucca once let slip that it was old Vegas money, but's that all he'd say. When they get nervous, these 'auditors' appear." Noah listened carefully, but Donny wasn't buying it.

Donny said, "All I know is that I didn't see a ring on Sis's finger. Well, at least the finger that matters."

Kartar shook his finger at Donny. "Listen to me! I'm pretty sure those two are a package, and regardless, they're dangerous! Stay away Donny."

Donny looked back at the office, wistfully.

"Donny, you need to take me seriously. And a word of advice about ad–wrapped vans . . ." Although it was clear Donny paid little attention, lost in daydreams of white leather jackets and blonde hair, Noah listened carefully.

#

No one saw either of the Lovers for the rest of the Sprint. Work didn't go very smoothly, because the hardware only arrived during the last three days of the Sprint when they'd planned to have it for eight. Noah's team planned to be the first to install onto hardware. During this time, the 'Scrum of Scrums' happened daily to see what could be done to help.

"Good thing we've been building automated tests," said Donny. "Between the automated unit tests and automated system tests, I know the app works. The BAs have been doing UAT with the simulator—"

"Exactly," Noah said. "SIMULATOR. We're going to look bad unless we get our installs on hardware."

Kartar waved at the barista for his usual. "How has support been?"

Noah tipped his head back and sighed. "English isn't their strong suit. Communication has been a disaster over the phone."

Kartar said, "Kong speaks Chinese. How about it Donny? Can you spare Kong?"

"How could I say no? LG says those auditors will attend the Demo, and I don't want to know what they're like when they have a genuine reason to be upset. I'll talk to Kong, and if he agrees, I'll convince Theckla to drop a user story since Kong'll be busy with Noah's team."

"It's worth a try," Noah said. "Without a breakthrough, we'll be demoing on the simulator again."

After their meeting, Kartar stayed at the coffee stand to reflect on how far they'd come. The simple philosophy of Agile had made fundamental changes in how everyone perceived contribution. It used to be that developers fought for design ideas, PMs fought for head count, and BAs fought for change requests. Stupid, unhelpful stuff, and now all that was gone. Something about having a year–long deadline left a lot of room for wasteful activities. Simply changing the release deadline to three months, along with the requirement to be potentially shippable, meant every Sprint transformed perceptions. There simply wasn't time to have documentation–heavy and meeting–heavy processes. Now everyone had business–facing features to deliver, and they couldn't succeed without the others. Even the old man had started coming to Daily Scrums and frequently consented to impromptu developer demos for his feedback.

But Lovers. . . . They were uncompromising. The only way out now would be to complete a release before they started killing people. Their bosses would call off the crusade once players started spending money playing the Winner.

On the night before Sprint end, Kong and Noah's team got the hardware working. Everyone was tired and wore out during the Sprint Demo, but even LG and Theckla stayed up late and supported them with manual testing, nonetheless Winner was running on hardware.

Like a kid at Christmas, DeLucca clutched one of the

rubberized chrome rectangles and played away at 'Slots,' often ignoring the presentation. While Prince talked about the work they did on UI gestures, DeLucca interrupted, jumping up and swearing, then bragging he'd just lost three hundred dollars. The Lovers sat quietly in the back, dressed like elitists from the movie Gattaca: both in all–white pant suits; Lex in a white jacket and pants with an oval neck cotton shirt; Sis in opal white gabardine pants and lab coat with large square–cut pockets, and a shirt with cubes of transparency hinting at haute couture. The Lovers left the Winners before them untouched. At the end of the hour, Sis requested a functional test traceability matrix.

"Take a photo of the build monitor," Kartar said. "The test reports are refreshed continuously."

"A photo can't be a system of record," she said. "It needs signatures for sign–offs." Then she turned to DeLucca and complained about Soxly compliance, and how her people wouldn't like the slipshod way things were being done. Noah got very busy typing on his phone and in moments, a fire drill interrupted the meeting.

"Kartar," Noah said on their way out. "I don't think facilities will keep doing that. They're starting to ask questions."

Kartar caught Noah's shoulder. "Did you see how excited DeLucca was? We just need to hang on long enough for our first release. Once the stakeholders see money coming in, anything those auditors say won't matter a damn."

Noah shielded his eyes from the sun. "Donny's with his team on the other side of the lot." Donny started toward them at Noah's wave.

Kartar said, "I hope you and Donny realize you need to take care with those two. Lovers aren't just with the PMI."

Noah's face, instead of registering surprise, only looked intent. "So, what are you trying to say?"

"They're professional killers."

Noah didn't blink. "You have evidence?"

His eyes seemed to probe for secrets to extract and judge. There was more to Noah than software architect.

"No," Kartar said.

"Come on! There must be something! Something DeLucca said, something the BAs have said. Some chatter you heard walking through the office."

The questions were off–putting, like an interrogation in the principal's office over an English paper.

Donny joined them. Kartar brushed back his pompadour, thought for a moment, then shook his head. "I've no further information. But I'd check your car if I were you."

Donny said, "Huh?"

"Yes. You both should check underneath for tracking devices or explosives."

"What?" said Donny. "Are you talking about Lovers again? You're too much." He walked away and gazed at the giant reproduction of Tansey's 'Triumph over Mastery' on De'Arte's outer walls: a modernist painter using a white roller brush to cover Michelangelo's mural in the Sistine Chapel.

Noah kept listening so Kartar continued. "And be careful about being alone in the parking garage. Their cover is an ad–wrapped van. If one tails you, go someplace public, and do it quick. Don't let them know where you live. Though they always seem to find out."

Noah listened with a focus that seemed to absorb every detail.

"You know," Donny said, still facing away, "Thekla was telling me about this painting. If the auditors paint over us with Waterfall, they'll only hurt themselves, just like Tansey's painter. I mean he's whitening out his own shadow for goodness sakes. He'll end up erasing himself."

Noah said to Kartar, "So how do you know all this?"

Kartar opened his sport jacket and Noah's eyes narrowed at the small nylon handgun tucked into a breast holster.

"I just know," Kartar said. "Look, I've got to go pick up my daughter."

Noah simply nodded and that bothered Kartar. How could Noah so cooly accept all that he'd said?

\#

Sis sat behind the wheel and used the rear–view mirror to work on her makeup. Lex sat in the other seat, making appreciative comments as Sis covered her lips with bright red lipstick, outlining them with an eyeliner pen so they really popped. Then she increased the definition of eyes and cheekbones, transforming her face from authoritative and commanding to dark, sultry, and impossible to ignore. She pulled her skirt's waistband high on her abs so the bottom edge hit just above mid–thigh. She took her shirt off and wore only a blazer, buttoned low so the black strap of her bra showed provactively.

"I love it when ye' go in sexy," said Lex. Her hand brushed Sis's thigh.

"I'll go first," said Sis. "Then, when his guard is down, drop a bag over his head."

\#

As Kartar had done every Friday since school had started, he left work early to get Dharma from the airport. It was opening weekend for the latest Star Trek, so after a quick stop to grab a bite, he drove them to the best theatre in town. She was quiet, texting a friend, sometimes a fit of laughter happened followed by flurries of thumb–typing. In those cases, he'd pester for an explanation and she'd look at him sideways, and more often than not, simply ignore him and go back to her phone. Other times, she'd share something of her life: a friend's interest in boys, a classmate's purchase of hip clothes and mascara, or how someone had their cell phone confiscated at school.

"It's the third time they've taken it from her," Dharma said, rolling her eyes. "She got the latest model. Her parents don't even know she has it. She bought it online and shipped it to a friend's, and now Mrs. Karens will turn it over to her parents. Her goose is so cooked!"

Then Dharma's phone would chime and she'd be back to double–thumb typing while he added yet another fiber to the tapestry of his daughter's life he kept in his heart.

His own phone rang and he took the call over the Caddy's hands–free system. "Hello?" he said.

There was a sharp intake of breath then a slow groan. Dharma looked up from her phone.

"Hello?" he repeated. The deepness of the groan over the Cadillac's high–fidelity sound system brought to mind an unpleasant picture. He switched off hands–free and held the handset to his ear.

"Dad, what are you—"

"Donny?" he said. He hadn't seen him since the fire alarm.

"Yeah," Donny croaked. Although in pain, he also sounded disappointed. "I broke. I told them the Gantt and WBS were nonsense. Sorry."

"Don't apologize! What the hell?! How messed up can they be to care more about reporting than the application —where are you Donny?"

"In my defense, this started out as a good night—"

"What are you talking about?"

". . . ended with me superglued to a chair."

"You serious? Just slip off your shirt and pants."

"I'm naked. My skin and hair are glued to a chair."

Kartar nearly hit the car ahead. "You're what? I'm calling the police."

There was fumbling on the other end and then Donny bellowed.

"Donny! What's happening?"

His cries died to panting words, "No. No. Oh no! No police."

Faintly there was whispering which Donny repeated. "You. Must. Come. And—"

Focused, he listened to everything that came through: soft, primal groans of pleasure or pain, the creak of leather, the crack of a whip, feminine whispers. It all came together. "I told you to stay away from that woman!"

"But you weren't there. She met me at my car, wearing red lipstick and—"

"I don't care what she was wearing! You didn't listen to a thing I said!"

"Come on! How was I supposed to know they were into S&M?"

"They? You were going to try and sleep with both of them? Donny! They're not into S&M, they're going to kill you!"

Dharma grabbed his arm. "Dad! Call the police!"

"No, no, no police!" Donny's words faded into moans. "You need to talk to them. Maybe if you talk to them, they'll understand. And bring acetone. I'm leaving behind enough skin as it is."

The connection died.

Dharma shouted, "Brake! Brake!"

Brake lights loomed. He stood on the brake, dropping

phone and bracing against the wheel with both hands. The hood dipped; Dharma, hands thrown forward, her body pressing into her seatbelt; Dharma's purse, Starbucks cups, and charging cables tumbling into footwells and windshield. The car stopped inches from the bumper.

Dharma stared at Kartar. "Who are you talking to? Why do you need to call the police?" She began dialing her phone.

"No!" He made a grab but she jerked it from reach. "Give it to me!" He leaned for it, arms stretched outward, seatbelt stopping him short.

"No, I will not!" Dharma pressed into her door, banged fist and phone into the window, then held her phone behind the seat. "I'm calling the police. Then I'm calling Mom about this S&M thing you've got going on."

His phone chimed the arrival of a text but the handset now lay beside the brake pedal. He took off his seatbelt and stretched for it. The traffic began to move. The guy behind them honked. He couldn't reach it.

"You listen to me! I'm your father and I forbid you from calling the police! Dharma. . . . If you've ever honored me, now's the time to just do what I say. This is very serious!"

She stopped stretching her arm to the back and sat normal, hugging phone to stomach, watching for sudden moves.

"Stop being so bossy! Focus on driving!"

Kartar spoke while wagging his finger. "Don't do anything! For a minute! Give me a minute!"

He drove, swerving across lanes, cutting off a Camaro, and entered a parking lot. There, he got out and fished his phone off the floor. His hands shook while he read the message, an address followed by: 'You have fifteen minutes!'

Kartar said nothing as he got back in the car, put on

his seatbelt, and drove. Dharma faced him, twisted sideways in the seat, ignoring her phone's chimes for attention.

"Dad, the cinema is the other way. Will you tell me what's wrong?"

Kartar wiped sweat from his nose. How could he bring his daughter close to danger? How could he abandon Donny? What the hell should he do?

Dharma set her hand on his arm. "Level with me. I've seen police shows. I can put it all together: the Cadillac, calls from disappointed clients about S&M, you won't call the police. Dad!" she said, pointing at him, "You're trafficking women!"

"Dharma! You just stop right there! I'm trying to think."

He needed to solve the problem of her being in the car within the next few minutes. Who could he call to take her? DeLucca? Too unpredictable. Thekla? She lived on the other side of town. LG? Although she was coming around, she'd want to call the cops. J? Nowhere to be found. That left only Noah, who had likely sold him out to the auditors in the past. But at least Noah took the Lovers seriously. Maybe he'd watch Dharma.

"Dad! I love you. I promise not to tell Mom you're a pimp, at least not right away, and—"

"Shush!" He dialed but Noah didn't answer. Into voicemail he said, "Call me if you can get to the Holiday Motel in short order. It's about that . . .," he glanced at Dharma, "impediment I told you about. Donny's in it up to his eyebrows."

"Dad, what's an impediment?"

Kartar shook his head. "The gods have spared no love for me."

He stopped in a parking lot within walking distance of the address, the Holiday Motel. It was a leftover from the seventies. At a glance, you could sense cheap carpeting, lumpy beds, and room doors that opened with oversized metal keys.

He gazed at the place. "There's always a way," he said. "You just need to be smart enough to see it. If there's anything I learned from J, it was—"

Across the street was the Stratosphere casino. The image of a blimp flickered across its jumbotron with an invitation to take the Vegas Blimp for a ride. The tower loomed above. At the top of concrete legs was a cylindrical pod of tourist fun.

He said, "You always wanted to ride the roller coasters at Disney Land. Did you know there's one on the Stratosphere?"

"But you always called them overpriced death machines."

"Well . . ." Yes, he'd said that, and the Strat was particularly expensive. Even a ride up the elevator cost money, and then everything at the top was ridiculously overpriced. However, up there, she'd be nearly out of reach.

Dharma squinted at him, her lips firming as she readied to argue. He held out two hundred dollars in twenties, an impressive bundle of bills.

"Go and play. I'll get Donny and come up in a few minutes."

Dharma snatched the money and fled. Once she'd safely entered the foot of the tower, he got out and opened the trunk.

#

There were basically two approaches, Kartar decided. Go in unarmed and be captured and eventually killed, or go in heavily armed, and make enough noise to attract police. The first option had a high probability of leading to the end of Donny as well. With the second, if he kept the Lovers busy enough, they might just leave Donny alone.

Shotgun or AR–15, one of life's tough decisions. Nothing's better than a shotgun for close quarters, but it's all but useless if the target is fifty feet away. Putting off the decision for a moment, he removed his concealed carry shoulder holster and set it in the trunk so he could armor up. He'd just got his head through the Kevlar vest when the roar of an engine had him turning around. A BMW with the license 'LNX LVR' framed with penguins sped toward him across the parking lot—Noah. Closer and closer the car came, not slowing. Panicking, Kartar scrambled to the opposite side of his car. Noah hit the brakes at the last second and somehow got the car to slide sideways, front bumper sliding to a stop not a foot from the side of the Cadillac, the two cars forming a neat 'T.'

Before Kartar started to breath again, Noah shouted as his window lowered, "Get down!"

Kartar dropped to the pavement. Noah ducked beneath his dash. A laser dot tracked across his windshield, then glass exploded.

Kartar lay still, scanning for a red dot, scared to move, his back itching like it was on fire.

"Noah?" he shouted.

No answer. Although every fiber of his being screamed for him to stay put, it would be sure death. The sniper would eventually move to another position and finish him.

A thud came from inside Noah's car.

"Are you hurt?" said Kartar.

"Uh–huh."

"Are you badly hurt?"

"Uh–huh. WDIWT? You had to park in the most

exposed location possible! Why?"

"Uh . . . because I don't know any better?"

"Could use a hand with bleeding. You know first aid?"

"There's a kit in my trunk. I'll call the police."

"Already coming," Noah said. "Helluva shot though. Got me through the dash."

Noah gasped and coughed for a while. "Lex has got to be ex–IRA. I've a leak that needs your help. So . . . so keep your head down."

Kartar rolled to the rear of his car, leapt up and dove into the trunk. The medical kit dug against his ear. He grabbed it and flopped back to the pavement, bruised his shoulder, cursed, and rolled to Noah's door. There, he stayed prone while pulling the door open. Noah lay on the floor, red blossoming around the hand pressed to his shoulder. Kneeling on the pavement, Kartar set the kit on the seat. There was a 9mm automatic on the floor.

"Ah, Noah. Who's gun?"

"So . . . I'm a feeb. I'm investigating organized crime."

"Feeb?"

"IT geeks!" Noah actually rolled his eyes. "I'm FBI."

Kartar shook his head. "You're FBI and an architect?"

Noah thumped his head against the floor. "Well, no shit! Do you think the FBI doesn't do any IT? Have you ever heard of Cyber Security? Are you going to help me stop the bleeding, or conduct a code review while the shooter maneuvers for a better shot!"

He cut Noah's shirt free and went to work cleaning and plugging the wound. The shot had exited out his back, so there were two wounds to bandage. Finished, Kartar wiped his hands clean and heard a helicopter approaching.

"Finally, the cavalry," Noah said.

Kartar shook his head. "You're really FBI?"

"Jesus! And they call us feebs!"

Kartar's phone rang. Although he had the earwig, he turned to look at the handset in his pocket. There was a plunk sound and a hole appeared in the car panel where his head had been.

"Shot!" yelled Noah.

Kartar rolled into the shadow of his car while Dharma's voice came over his earwig.

"Dad! I'm on the observation deck. You're so weird today. You look like you're stealing that car."

"Dharma!"

"I really don't get you today. It's like I've never known you. These binoculars are major awesome! I can see—Oh God! Is that man bleeding?!"

"Dharma! You shouldn't be watching this!"

Shots slammed the pavement below his feet and something cut across his face.

"Dad! A woman with a gun is coming!"

Noah yelled, "The sniper is trying to flush you from cover."

"Where is she?" Kartar asked Dharma. He tucked his knees close, backed against the bumper and looked around, ears straining for telltale sounds of Irish music, but couldn't. The sound of the chopper got louder.

"She running from the motel—run Dad! She's almost there!"

He must leave. But Noah . . . .

"Dad," Dharma squealed. "She's going to see you!"

He scrambled around to the driver's side and squatted with back against the door, trying to spot the approaching woman.

"Dad, you've got to go!" pleaded Dharma.

Kartar got behind the wheel and started the car. The windshield exploded, and he could see nothing. It's lights out, he thought. I'm dead. Then he noticed light leaking in at the edges of his vision. In another heartbeat, he discovered the sun visor had been split in two and hung dangling over his face.

Brushing the visor away, he put the car in drive and pealed out, trunk lid slamming shut. Hunched low, he swerved hard enough to have fallen out of the seat if not for clutching the wheel. He ducked below the dash, anticipating a shot.

"She's still after you Dad! Behind you!"

Over the sidewalk and off the curb, the car bounced into traffic. He swerved to miss a motorcycle and cut off a pickup with longhorns on its hood. Ahead loomed the concrete legs of the Stratosphere. He aimed the car across all lanes of traffic and drove directly to the valet stand. Before valets appeared, he jumped from the car and fast walked for the entrance, the vehicle still running.

Sis, in a black suit skirt and the same red wig she wore when she murdered him on the monorail, ran after him in black sneakers. She waved at the traffic and crossed in the same place he had.

He glanced back at his black Caddy, longing for the weapons in the trunk. But he'd be exposed. She'd pick him off. And he wouldn't be able to enter the casino. The valet held the car door and stared at the windshield fragments littering the front seats for about ten seconds, then got in and took it to parking.

"Dad! Where are you? She's crossing the street."

Kartar entered the Stratosphere, white shirt collar sticking cockeyed from the neck of the Kevlar vest. He ran through the lobby to the tower section, and pushed through the tourists in line to buy elevator passes. None resisted his pushing past. Perhaps the black vest gave him an aura of authority, as if he was staff security.

While the clerk ran his card, he looked back and saw

Sis shoving her way through the line. A bald biker grabbed her arm as she passed. She pivoted, reversed his hold, and twisted his arm up and behind his back. His friends watched in surprise while she propelled him forward, using him as a battering ram through the remaining tourists, keeping her hold on his arm until she bought a ticket and left him behind.

Kartar cut the line to the security checkpoint. The bored attendant barely blinked at his vest, but held him up to empty pockets and remove the earwig before allowing him to pass through the detection arch.

The Stratosphere used double decker elevators. After the top cabin loaded, the doors closed and the car moved up one floor to allow the boarding of the bottom cabin. The line moved fast. He quickly collected his things and pushed past couples discussing brochures and parents with kids pulling their arms. He'd have reached the front too, except for a barricade of Italians standing shoulder–to–shoulder marveling at the sexy Vampirella meets Cirque De Soli poster on the elevator door. He leaned into the group and watched for Sis.

"Give it up," he said to himself. "You can't bring your gun. Just go home. You won't get me this time."

Sis stepped to the side of the line to gauge the checkpoint, then followed in the wake of a family of six. After the kids passed through, she pointed past the attendant and said something. When the attendant turned, she slid the handbag over the floor so it passed the detection arch on the outside. Then she stepped through the arch and, before the attendant's attention returned, she'd grasped the handle on the top of the bag and walked peremptorily toward Kartar.

"Shit," Kartar said, putting the earwig back on.

"What is it?" asked Dharma.

"Nothing," he said.

Sis sped past a teenage boy focused on his iPad. Finally, the elevators door opened and everybody pressed forward.

She tapped the shoulder of an overweight tourist with a Vegas T–Shirt stretched over his beer belly. When he turned to look over his shoulder, she darted past on the opposite side. Kartar pulled his toes out of the doorway, leaned back into people as hard as he could, and punched furiously at the 'Close Doors' button. Sis closed in fast, her bag's Prada logo flashing with its gold finish. The doors finally responded but stopped at an Adidas in the threshold. With his own foot, Kartar swept the sneaker out of the way and punched the door switch again. Before the doors closed, Sis mouthed the words, "I will get you."

#

Kartar started to breathe again as the elevator rose, but only half a breath because the car suddenly stopped, its display showing: 'Loading bottom car.'

The bit of metal beneath his feet was all that separated him from Sis.

Sweat slicked his forehead as the certainty that it was all about to happen again weighed on him. Life was down to seconds, maybe minutes. This would be the last moment of peace before she killed him, like the time he commuted home with the painted desert sky looming before him, or the time he carried the poster from the printers through the busy streets of Vegas. This time, his last view would be of foreign tourists in designer labels mixed with tawdry Vegas apparel. Soon Sis would be chasing, shooting, and murdering. At any second, she could start firing through the elevator floor.

"Soon it'll be over," he said.

He squeezed past the others to press himself firmly

against a wall. A young woman in leather short–shorts and oversized Italian sunglasses gave him a quizzical look.

"Scusami? Signore? Are you OK?"

He wanted to collapse. How could this be going so wrong when so much had gone right? The team delivered automatically–tested enhancements each Sprint, they rarely needed to spend resources fixing regressions, and they could actually ship what they had built. But these . . . idiots couldn't see beyond their reports. J had mentioned organizational antibodies, and had said the best way to combat them was to show results. Within weeks they would go live with V1.0. Why couldn't they trust just a little longer?

Everybody was looking at him, many speaking to each other in Italian. The young woman's burly boyfriend set a hand on Kartar's shoulder and asked, "Are you OK?" All Kartar could do was stare at the words "Italia" on the man's jacket, trying not to have a full–blown panic attack.

Kartar pinched the ring on his necklace while wondering why Sis was stuck in an infinite loop of Waterfall. Why wouldn't a PMI poo–bah let them do something different?

Something was deeply wrong.

It wasn't just a woman or a killer he fled, but an idea as well. An idea that those who didn't do the work and who were above collaboration, should dictate how the work was performed. By demanding certain reports, they enforced a specific way of development. Some time ago, Waterfall had stopped being optimal if it ever had been. Sis was smart, put–together, and disciplined, but she'd stopped thinking. And she wasn't alone, because he and the PMs, BAs, and business managers had all been in the same space. Something had happened across the entire software industry, and he was going to be murdered by conventionalism. He'd be shot for trying something new, something that extended beyond doing engineering into how it was done.

Conventional development could not save the Winner. To change was to survive, but habits always fight change. The changes made to save the product had triggered an organizational reaction, one which viewed what he'd done as dangerous rather than helpful—no, what they'd done. This time he wasn't alone, and so far, the Lovers had captured Donny, shot Noah, and within seconds, the elevator will deliver him to the most important person in the world and—.

She's going to see her father murdered, he realized. He pushed through the crowded elevator and punched every button that could possibly send it back down. But its course, along with his fate, was set. Resigned, he rested his head on the bulkhead until something even worse came to mind: he may see his daughter killed.

"Signore? You ill?"

He turned to the boyfriend and the strapping man's face hardened at what he saw in Kartar's and turned away. Kartar faced the doors and vowed that, no matter what, he'd throw himself and Sis from the top of the Stratosphere before allowing her harm to his Dharma.

Behind him came the noise of energetic conversations in Italian.

He spoke to his earwig, "Dharma—"

"You don't sound OK."

"I'm not. I'm in elevator 2. Meet me at the inside observation deck."

"I'm at the door. You're nearly here."

"Be ready."

"For what Dad?"

The doors opened to a glass–walled observation room with a reddening sunset bloodying dark storm clouds in the distance. Hundreds of tourists crowded together to fit on the needle's tip that was the Stratosphere tower, shooting selfies and groupies. Couples queued for empty corners to pose and smile. A tour group walked the circumference in a clockwise fashion, deliberating the sights in German.

And there was Dharma.

He cut through several people's photos to enfold her in his arms. He held her close and guided her from the elevator. Her beside him, her presence, her smell, her soul. No devastation would be greater than to live and to see her die. Failure to keep her protected would follow him no matter how many more lives he lived. Such incompetence would haunt him forever.

Behind a round coffee–shop table, he pulled her to squat beside, watching over the tabletop for Sis.

The Italians had finally all exited. Seconds passed while people loaded the empty elevator. He waited, hand on Dharma's shoulder, her wide eyes bearing questions he had no time to answer.

The elevator's display read 'Other deck being served' and in moments, the doors closed and it descended.

Kartar straightened. "Where is she?"

"Who?" Her eyes darted whichever direction he looked.

"The woman. Sis. She was in the lower cabin."

"That part exits at the bar below," said Dharma. She began to bit her nails.

"Bad enough when I can see her coming. Even worse when she could come from anywhere. Come. We've got to move."

The tip of the Stratosphere was shaped like a giant spinning top, six floors with outside walls of man–sized panes of glass containing: a chapel, corporate meetings rooms, a restaurant, nightclubs, a lower observation floor boasting the world's highest Starbucks, and then on the roof was the upper observation deck that overlooked the Strip. The upper observation deck, really nothing more than a patio and waiting area for attractions where good money was spent to have oneself whisked, dropped, or thrown to the brink of annihilation.

Towering red mesa clouds were now the only traces of the sun, and everywhere were lines of excited daredevils and hanger–ons from all parts of the world, waiting for their ride or to watch loved ones scream like children. Take any seaside carnival and select the three rides most guaranteed to finish in disaster if a handful of rivets came loose, and those were the rides perched in precarious positions a thousand feet above the ground. The X Scream, which started its journey as a nonchalant rollercoaster car any gray haired mum would enjoy, suddenly veered over the edge of the building in simulated track failure. Another was the Insanity, an "egg beater with seats" that coaxed gentle people to relax on its upholstery, then with victims entrapped in its clutches, spirited them over the guardrail and spun them in a circle at forty miles–per–hour until their brains were scrambled. The Sky Jump, nothing more than a practice session for those bent on ending it all with a leap. Nearly every participant that stood at the precipice required several moments of gentle consoling by the ride attendant (and less gentle ribbing by onlookers). Nervous hands betrayed adventurous hearts until the attendant, due to some innate roadside wisdom and compassion, coaxed them to jump. The entire way down the victim screamed gloriously, spread eagle like an angel who'd lost its wings, only held in check by two cables the thickness of a pinky until alighting at the tower's base.

"That's a neat trick," Kartar said to Dharma. "Now she'll have to buy another elevator ticket to come back up."

"Dad, what did you mean about 'that woman?' The way you talk, it sounds like you know her."

He prepared something evasive yet honest, like that he knew her from a previous life. But a sudden hiss of pneumatics distracted Dharma into looking overhead, at the needle tower placed atop the Stratosphere. As if rides like the X Scream, Insanity, and Sky Jump just might not be enough, they'd added one more—the Big Shot. A couch attached to a pneumatic piston that rocketed you and three friends at four Gs up the additional sixteen stories to the needle's tip. Then, after a brief pause to take in the city skyline and gulp a bit of air, the couch dropped, plummeting back to the start and braking with a loud hiss.

"Rides are closing folks!" shouted an attendant, an Asian woman too young to be a college grad, yet too seasoned to not have started—probably took a year off or had dropped out. Looking official, radio strapped across her chest, she announced the early closing was due to an approaching storm. She certainly had her work cut out persuading distracted and disappointed tourists to give up the otherworldly neon landscape that brightened the darkness below.

Kartar allowed him and Dharma to be herded along with the rest of crowd leaving the upper deck via the elevator. Inside the observation room, Sis watched all who queued for an elevator.

"Come," Kartar said and broke away.

The attendant tried for their attention but Kartar ignored her and followed the circumference of the patio until they were out of view. The air smelled of dusty cactus, traffic, and moisture. All of the world seemed distant and too far below to be a bother. But the "whup–whup" of a helicopter broadcasted the problems of a world that wished him ill: Donny was trapped, Noah was shot, he was being hunted and Dharma was in danger.

Two blocks distant, the helicopter hovered over the parking lot, its spotlight gliding over the roofs of nearby houses and motels.

Kartar said, "That car you thought I was stealing? Inside was a bleeding man. Did he get help?"

Dharma nodded. "When you were in the elevator. And just like on TV, their clothes had F.B.I. on their backs and chest."

"So Noah really is a . . . Feeb."

Dharma put her back to the city to face him. "Why was that woman chasing you Dad?"

Hard to decide where to start. Or how much to share. "She's from work."

"What? A coworker wants to shoot you?! Because?"

"She's upset about Winner. Dharma, you must leave with the others. She probably doesn't know about you. Even if she does, I doubt she'd spot you in the crowd."

Dharma frowned, head hanging back to look at him like they discussed her being grounded. "What've you done?" She gnawed at a nail until he pulled her hand down.

"Right now, things are outstanding. Better than ever actually! But there's a reporting mismatch." He sighed and stared out over the neon city. "She's thinks her reports are the cat's meow—more indicative than the results. She wants 'productivity theater' to represent productivity rather than completed work. But her reports are not process agnostic. They require us to work in the wrong ways."

Dharma's head shook through the last part, as if she didn't quite catch it.

"Hold on!" The lights of Vegas reflected in her widening eyes. "She's upset enough to shoot at you over paperwork? That's insane!"

He hung onto the rail and squatted, resting forehead onto cool metal, staying this way while he spoke. "She's followed me up here, and that's a good thing, because they've got Donny trapped. If she's chasing me, she's not hurting him. But you—." He looked up at her. "You've got to get out of here."

Of all the places on Earth loaded with distractions, the Stratosphere of Las Vegas must be in the top five, so it was no wonder he hadn't noticed it until now. For a moment, he thought he'd actually gone insane because there was a four–story face of Agile consultant J staring at him from the other side of the roof. From the front, the blimp was oval like a face, the top the same Autobot blue as J's hair with a red dot at the center of the forehead for his god mark. Above the dot were the same yellow grill lines as on J's forehead.

If that wasn't a sign from the gods, then none existed.

Dharma noticed what caught his attention. "No! I know that look—No Dad! Don't even think—"

"Come! I know how we're going to get away from here."

"DAD—" Dharma stamped her foot and crossed arms just like when she was seven and had been told to go to bed. "You can't pilot that! We both go down the elevator with everyone else."

"She's waiting for that. She knows we'll have to leave. But no one would think of the blimp."

He grabbed her arm and pulled her to where the blimp was unobscured by amusement rides. It was over fifty yards long. Metallic blue ran the length of its top. The sides were white with the word's "Getting Agile?" painted along its side, the question mark in the shape of a tree with branches bent in a wind. Agile Tree, J's company. He tried to pull her to the gangplank but she resisted, grabbing the patio handrail with one hand and his arm with the other.

"You'll get us both killed! And if we do survive, I'm telling Mom and she'll kill you!"

"I'll live with that."

He pulled again and she wrapped both arms and legs around the railing stanchion, hugging herself to it. At the tower top they battled, their background a velvety darkness disrupted by a glowing Excalibur castle, an Egyptian Sphinx, and flashes of every color in the spectrum powered by fifteen thousand miles of neon tubing. Kartar struggled with Dharma, wrapping arms around her like she was a body pillow and pulling with all his might, each pleading for the other to stop because the other would get them killed. Both gasping and sweating in a titanic battle of stubbornness.

#

Kartar and Dharma spied on Sis as she finally gave up waiting in the observation room and came out to find Kartar. Sis walked the patio, acting as if she had misplaced a friend, keeping a benign and befuddled expression while passing between the rollercoaster and the 'egg beater.' She moved slowly and looked into each shadow stretching between patio lights. Kartar held his breath and hoped an attendant would notice and escort her down—the simplest way of being rid of her. No one else was on the patio. A crowd queued within the glass walls of the observation deck, their attentions on the elevator or entering the lower floors. He and Dharma crouched behind the rollercoaster, watching Sis move closer to the blimp.

"Come on Dad," said Dharma. "They aren't going to notice her. She looks too . . . classy. Dressed like that, everyone assumes she's where she's supposed to be." She gripped his bicep, her nails digging into his skin. "Do it."

"There are two ropes holding it in place. I'm not sure there's time."

She rolled her eyes then mimed choking him. "You and Mom spent all that money on sailing lessons—"

"Her idea!"

Dharma nodded. "Just follow the plan. Even with your awful idea, you'd have to plan on untying it."

"But—," his protest stopped because Dharma thrust her finger at him.

He unmuted his earwig and said, "Wh–Why you doing this?" He spoke the words facing away so his words wouldn't carry. Then he turned to watch.

Sis darted to the blimp's gangplank. "How about you come out so we can talk Mr. Patel." She walked slowly now, one hand holding the top handle of her bag, the other rested inside.

Again Kartar spoke, facing away. "How about you leave. The FBI is right outside." His earwig transmitted his words to Dharma's phone, and her phone loudly echoed the words from its position in the blimp's cabin, its volume set to high.

Sis studied the blimp, appraising the gangway connecting patio to cabin. "We'll do things my way."

Kartar and Dharma froze in place as Sis looked in their direction, then she walked up the gangplank.

"Hey, you two shouldn't be here!"

Dharma and Kartar jumped at the voice. The Asian woman with the radio had come up from behind.

Sis squatted at the cabin entrance and waited, barely visible through the nylon webbing along the gangplank's side.

"Go talk to her," Kartar whispered, pushing Dharma toward the attendant. He stayed hidden behind the rollercoaster, willing Sis to enter the blimp.

Dharma approached her. "Sorry. We're lost."

The attendant gave her a 'No shit you're lost' look. "What about your friend? Didn't you hear the PA?"

Kartar cursed to himself as Sis still hadn't moved. The attendant was screwing everything up. Why couldn't she have caught Sis instead?

The attendant spoke into her radio. "I've got two stragglers by the coaster. Save me an elevator." Dharma continued walking toward the attendant who clicked the mic off and waved at Kartar. "Hey mister! Come on!"

Kartar darted in a crouch past the rollercoaster car. In ten steps, he had reached the rope that moored the blimp's bow. The line was taut. He pulled hard to slip it off the spar, but couldn't get enough slack. A wind whistled through the tower and the blimp shifted. He struggled again with the line for a few seconds, then rolled across the floor. Something ricocheted nearby. On hands and knees, he focused on the gangplank instead and gave it a hard shake. Sis swayed, one hand gripping the gun, the other on the handrail. Somehow, the opposite side of the gangplank was well–fixed to the cabin.

He rolled back to the bowline, and with both hands, pulled the line. He got some slack, then pulled some more, the loop slipped close to the end of the spar, and stuck there. She fired. His arm went numb. Sis rushed him as the line finally slipped off the spar; he pushed the gangplank which, in turn, pushed the nose of the blimp away from the Stratosphere. The wheels of the gangplank rolled to the edge of the platform, and the gap between blimp and building increased. Sis staggered on the unsteady ramp and brought her gun level with Kartar's head as one foot of the plank rolled off the building.

The plank twisted sideways, Sis fell, and Kartar dove from her aim.

She dangled in the air between blimp and Stratosphere, both hands wrapped in webbing. The red wig hung on her shoulder for a moment until a breeze nudged it away. The end of the gangplank listed a full forty–five degrees, one foot still clinging to the deck, Sis hanging in the middle.

"You're bleeding!" Dharma said.

Kartar looked down at himself. Blood spread down the shoulder of his shirt and he didn't feel well.

The attendant who'd been shouting all hell into her radio became quiet.

"Is that a gunshot wound? There's a shooter?" At Kartar's nod, the woman made a choking sound and ran for the elevators. Dharma looked at him, stunned.

Kartar took his daughter by the shoulder and said, "We need to finish the job and get the blimp away. She's too dangerous. She'll kill us as we leave the building if we don't. You push the plank." He showed her how, grabbing the patio handrail with one hand and pushing the gangplank handrail with the other. "I'll get the aft line free. That should send it sailing downwind."

Kartar rushed to the rear of the blimp. Something about the lights, or maybe the wind pushing at him, made him dizzy.

"Hurry!" Dharma shouted. "She's pulling herself onto the plank."

The aft line was slack and easily slipped off the mooring, but a brisk wind pushed the blimp into the tower.

"Push!" he shouted.

"It isn't moving!" She shouted and then suddenly backed away.

"What are you doing?" Kartar shouted and then saw that Sis no longer dangled. The plank was completely sideways because she'd managed to pull herself on top.

She crawled along the edge of the gangway toward the Stratosphere, where one foot of the gangplank still rested. She had a small handgun aimed at Dharma.

"No! No! No!" Kartar shouted, running toward his daughter. "Don't be rash! She's not involved."

"My dear friend," Sis said. "You try and drop me off the Stratosphere and now you worry I'll do something rash. You're a cute one Elvis."

He was in arms reach of Dharma when Sis halted him with her words: "Hold it up."

"Dad, she's going to shoot us." Dharma's eyes were wide open and focused on him, incredulous.

He should have left her safe in the Bay Area. Shouldn't have flown her in. Should've resisted seeing her. Should have—.

He held up his hands. "Let's not be hasty here. We can all get what we need. I'll go with you quietly. We can go talk to Donny. Dharma can take a cab home."

"Or I could just kill you now. Though with you alive, your daughter will be easier to manage as collateral until I can kill you at a more convenient time. The FBI is trying to ruin our day, it would seem."

Dharma shook her head. "How could you want to kill someone because of something at work? I mean, who does that?"

Sis smiled. "You've quite a girl there Kartar." She crawled near to the tower then said, "To put it simply, your father's Agile has put the inmates in charge of the asylum, and he must atone. Keep still while I get off this damn—"

"Acha. What a place!"

Kartar didn't see who it was that spoke until Dharma pointed upward. The blimp's top was three stories overhead, and there, above the words 'Getting Agile?,' was J peering over the ballooning sides.

"My sleep is disturbed even when on a blimp." J's long steel blue hair stuck out in all directions except the left side, pressed flat from sleeping. The wind stopped whistling and the blimp stopped pressing against the tower.

Despite the distraction, Sis stayed focused. Her eyes widened, but never left Kartar and Dharma. She was nearly to the Stratosphere but the last bit would require her to straddle or belly crawl across the part still hung on the patio, and she'd need both hands to do that.

J continued complaining. "Eh? This was to be a quiet and solitary job, yet here I have bombastic guests."

He scooted forward as if to see better, Kartar's breath catching in his throat when the little man began sliding headfirst. But J must've caught a handhold because his descent stopped abruptly.

"Acha? Kartar? And that your daughter! Congratulations!"

J smiled so wide his metallic blue sideburns were no longer visible. "You're finally spending time with the girl! This improves your karma immensely."

Kartar's head throbbed and he wanted to sit. Strange that the gunshot wound to his shoulder didn't hurt nearly as badly as when shot in the knee. Still, it was just like J to yammer on like Ma about ancient Hindu gotra lineage while he bled to death.

"Gods, you're such a jerk! You had me writing on those leaves—"

"You did that? See! The act of journaling helped you solve your own problems."

"I expected you to respond!"

"They're leaves Kartar. How can that work?"

Kartar groaned. "I knew it! You never received them! Of course you didn't. That was a canned response! I'm going to die. Again. And—"

J used hands to pull his lips apart and make a face at Kartar. His funny face changed to one of panic as something gave and he slipped down the blimp head first, hands scrambling for a hold. Dharma screamed as the strange man slid down the blimp's side, headed for a thousand foot fall. Kartar stepped forward, but there was nothing he could do.

J jerked to a stop, ten feet above the patio and hung upside down, bobbing from a safety line that connected him to a black harness belted over brown Carhartts.

"Acha, I'm glad I remembered that."

Kartar hollered half–remembered insults in Hindi until he got dizzy, then finished with, "When I die from this gunshot, I'm going to haunt the hell out of you!"

J tisked him. "It's only a nick. Although you could die from tetanus, I suppose." He twisted his body until he spun himself around to see Sis. "Gods! What has happened to the plank?! You're going to get me in trouble."

Wagging his body like a pendulum, J swung himself against the blimp and caught a line that ran vertically against its side. He righted himself, hooked a knee around the line, unclipped the safety line, and slid down the rope to the cabin door. At the threshold, he looked at Sis who glanced back, then he entered the cabin. From the dark interior came a cacophony of cans being knocked over, along with a string of creative swearing in Hindi.

"Friend of yours?" Sis said, trying to watch everyone.

After the cabin lights came on, J reappeared in the doorway standing before the gangplank, a vivid splotch of paint, the color of 'Getting Agile,' dripping down his coveralls.

"Who has abused this plank? And why is that woman pointing a gun at you?"

Kartar took a step toward Dharma but backed away at

a gesture from Sis. "She's one of the organizational antibodies you warned me about."

"She's going to kill Dad!"

Sis sat up on her knees, perhaps preparing to leap for it or maybe to negotiate with J. The plank wobbled while she raised her free hand. "Whoever you are, hang on until I get off this."

"Acha, like I told you, the best thing to do with such antibodies is to get them on your side. Otherwise it's an uphill battle and—"

"But she's got a gun!" shouted both Kartar and Dharma.

A moist gust swept over the patio and a flash of lightning in the distance strobed the carnival rides. The blimp shifted and the foot of the plank slipped closer to the precipice. Sis flattened, keeping the gun pointing forward, and worked her free hand and feet into the webbing. Kartar dashed to the gangway, put his heel to the footer, and shoved.

The footer slid off the edge and plummeted, and Sis hung upside down, hanging on with hands and feet. The gangway's opposite side stayed hooked to the cabin so that she hung vertically, her gun plunging the thousand feet to the concrete below.

J braced his hands against the doorjamb as the blimp lurched, leaning out to see what had happened as the blimp floated away. He seemed happy to see that Sis still hung from the gangway.

"Ahoy!" J called to Kartar. "I and the beautiful woman will have a nice chat over hot chai, and see if we can't come to an agreement. In the end, you either change your organization or you change your organization."

He disappeared into the cabin momentarily, then returned to call to Sis, "Miss, can you help me? Somewhere in here is an operator's manual." Then the wind picked up and thrust the blimp into the night.

LIBERATION & LIBATIONS

De'Arte's floor was filled with guests holding a Winner. The rollout started at night with L.A. hipsters, handsome men and beautiful women sitting at the blackjack tables, drinks in one hand, playing slots on the Winner with the other. Then at 6AM, the elderly couples crowding the breakfast buffets were carrying Winners and debating about whose handset was running hotter, often trading the units with friends by the time their steak and eggs or flapjacks and grits arrived. Then the families arrived. Mom and Dad played upright slot machines while their kids sat beside them on a stool, a Winner in their little hands, trying to run a streak.

It's the first twenty–four hours of operations for the Winner. A skeleton crew of Ka–ching, Wow, and Agent Smith pulled an all–nighter to analyze what their metrology features were telling them. The build monitor was repurposed to show live analytics generated by the players. As morning expired thousands of games had been played, and there was a healthy amount of data.

Thekla and LG huddled with a developer to discuss winner–loser ratios, and what games were popular among what players and wrote new user stories for the product backlog. Rockstar was relaxing in another chair, gazing at LG while she worked, a certain gleam in his eyes as he studied her.

"It's Now?" Kartar blurted. "You're finally into her now?"

Rockstar startled, blushed, then put his phone to ear, feigning he'd received a call from his bookie.

"Everyone!" DeLucca had returned from the floor. With a big smile, he led waiters with trays of champagne and breakfast into the teams' area. Although only ten AM, it was Vegas baby, and everybody was excited.

They gathered around the trays and each grabbed a glass of champagne as DeLucca made a toast.

"Well, this is first time I've done a 'soft launch,' " he said. "Originally, I envisioned a big launch with the Rockettes, Cirque de Soli, etc, but—"

He raised his glass to everyone in the room, and everyone raised theirs. "To think, we went from a twelve–month release to releasing every three months. Our stakeholders are unbelievably ecstatic to see us earning revenue nine months early. This, my friends, is epic! Here! Here!" Everybody echoed him, and everybody drank.

Kartar elbowed Donny in the back who winced. "Take it easy! I've still got scabs. You don't see me poking you in the shoulder."

"At least you didn't go skiing." Kartar tipped his glass toward Noah, whose arm was still in a sling and could barely leave his chair. Skiing in Taos was Noah's cover story for missing a week of work. His own wound had been, luckily, a simple emergency room visit.

"True, I didn't go to Taos. I didn't lose blood like

Noah, but I lost a truckload of pride. And I'd reckon pride has the longest road to recovery. That makes me the unsung hero of it all."

Kartar threatened to jab him.

"Hey!" Donny said. "I thought she was into me." Then he leaned close and mouthed the words: Noah a Fed? "I never would've guessed with all that sencha lotion and penguin worship."

Kartar nodded. "Me neither. Him bringing the calvary saved our asses, and here I thought he was tapping our phones to rat me out to—" Kartar stopped, realizing Donny wouldn't know about the times Kartar suspected Noah was betraying him to Lovers.

"What? The FBI was tapping our phones?"

Kartar nodded. "Usual for an organized crime investigation. I'm glad Noah's still here. DeLucca needs looking after until the court date. And Noah's genuinely excited to stay on a bit longer to see how Agile transforms the business."

Donny shook his head. "Damn! I bet it's so he can keep drawing two paychecks. Now that would be the life!"

"Maybe. You've got to be willing to go 'skiing.' I've got a teenaged daughter. I don't need any more excitement than that."

A wistful look came over the big man's face. "I believe Sis and Lex are still at large."

Kartar leveled a finger at Donny. "No man! Don't even go there!"

Donny laughed. "Never mind." He clinked Kartar's glass. "Agile hasn't just transformed the business, it's transformed the people too."

Kartar nodded. "I'll drink to that!"

It was a lot of work of course, and everyone had changed how they worked together; from developers doing TDD, making quality part of their daily production and minimizing cross team dependencies, to the business interacting with teams on a daily basis. Every aspect was necessary. Everyone had to engage each other in more effective ways, such as face–to–face communication in Daily Scrum, Sprint Planning, Sprint Retrospectives, and the Sprint Demo.

The old methods were too change–resistant to be successful in a dynamic world. The IT industry had been doing the same process for so long, Waterfall was institutionalized due to generations of management experience. Because the difference between Waterfall and Agile was so drastic, Agile seemed almost alien in comparison. If he'd learned anything from his past lives, it was that organizational transformation was hard. In the first Agile attempt, although they did Daily Scrum and could check off all the boxes for Scrum, they weren't Agile at all. He completely controlled his team, Thekla couldn't be a substitute for a supporting business, teams that were organized to make a pretty organization chart had tons of dependencies and technical impediments.

Kartar got another glass of bubbly. There was an imperceptible part to Agile. Doing the process only enabled agility. But it couldn't make you Agile. Like Donny said, 'being Agile' meant changing people. And not just the development team, or just the analysts, or just the management or business—Agile meant everyone being willing to change how they did work to support better product delivery.

Doing some things Agile and ignoring other aspects because they seemed 'too hard,' was like making a table with one or two legs. A 'half transformation' didn't solve many problems, so the ROI for 'half changed' wasn't good. Like when only his team did Scrum, and couldn't deliver fully working software. The Winner had too many challenges to succeed with just 'half' Agile.

The moment enough people felt threatened by changes, organizational antibodies appeared in the form of resistant BAs, commanding Directors, passive–resistant developers, and even aggressively–resistant stakeholders. Step by step along the value chain, from a single development team to across all teams, to the business itself—when the transformation transcended from something he needed into something that everyone wanted, they went beyond 'checkbox' Agile to being Agile. Now that the Winner was out there—had manifested itself—even the most ardent naysayer was seeing results. It never would have happened if they'd attempted to release in twelve, or even six months, because taking so long with an alien process required more faith than the organization had.

After this visible success, it'd be easier. With each release, they would develop new habits, and Agile—adapting to change for the business's competitive advantage—would become De'Arte's de rigueur.

Noah beckoned to Kartar. Kartar walked over and joined him, taking a seat beside Noah so they could talk at eye level.

Noah held out his hand and they shook in congratulations. "I've been thinking about how we're doing quarterly releases. But maybe we could do better."

Kartar nodded. "I want to propose we go to shorter Sprints. Two weeks is the typical length for mature Agile teams. Maybe we should try one week."

"I'll do you one better. How about deploying to prod as soon as a story is finished?"

"Eh?"

"During my convalescence, I did some reading about DevOps and Continuous Delivery."

Kartar stared blankly, not recognizing the terms.

Noah slapped his own forehead. "Come on! It's the latest Agile! Scrum's basic. It just inserts requirements, planning, and testing into iterative cycles. eXtreme Programming goes further with proscriptive details on how to do development. Then add Continuous Delivery, and it's like warp drive! It adds Agile to operations and deployments, and DevOps is the culture of how we get there."

Kartar's mouth hung open but he didn't know what to say.

Noah grinned. "You didn't think Scrum was the 'final revolution,' did you? Kartar, you've got to stay up to date! Don't fall from the bleeding edge!"

Kartar gazed pointedly at Noah's bandaged shoulder and they both laughed.

Noah gestured at the build monitor showing their tests in a green state. "We could be shipping each feature as soon as they pass the QA process. We create a pipeline from requirements, development, and then to production! I mean quarterly releases? Really? WDIWT?"

"Who's dumb idea was that? I'm going to punch you in the shoulder and the mouth."

"Kartar!" Thekla ran across the room, champagne sloshing from her glass, her face a little flushed. "There's someone waiting for you on the floor!"

Kartar shot out of his chair, mind racing as to who it might be.

"Uh . . . a new auditor?" He looked at Noah who shrugged. Outside of DeLucca, Noah, Donny, and himself, the office didn't know the Feds were investigating De'Arte's stakeholders.

Thekla laughed and patted his shoulder. "No, we haven't seen Lovers. It's a strange looking Indian fellow. Not handsome like you. He says he's a reporter . . . for Wired."

Although his mouth hung open, he didn't breathe.

Thekla patted his back. "Are you choking?"

"No, no, I'm OK." He gripped the ring through his shirt.

"Why aren't you running for the door? You always talk about getting on the cover of Wired."

He tried to decide if it really was a reporter, or just J playing some game.

Thekla handed him a business card. It was paper, and on it was a name, email address, and phone number.

"Got to go!" he said, smiling. "But just in case, tell Donny to come find me if I'm not back in an hour."

Thekla shook her head. "Living in Vegas has done something to you."

"That it has," agreed Kartar, and he ran to the casino floor.

AGILE DEVELOPMENT IS ABOUT HAVING FUN!

by Ebin John Poovathany

One of my friends Rakesh recently asked me, "What do you do in office?"

Given the fact that he has a finance background and not from IT industry, it took extra thought to answer "I help teams to increase their fun at work."

He looked baffled and said, "I never thought that someone would pay anyone to do that. I always thought that software development is a very tough and hectic job, and you feel very tired and exhausted at the end of the day."

I doled out a few more amazing facts. "Of course, not. We listen to music while working, we have unlimited supply of coffee and tea, are highly paid, have access to YouTube, we're always connected to internet and social media, almost all the time we are doing new things, and yes, we do spend a great amount of time in meetings and discussions. In addition to all of that, we have flexible work hours and can work from wherever we want. What more you can ask for?"

I chuckled at his bemused look and then he said, "Seems like real fun!" He pondered over something on his mind then asked, "So if they are already having fun, then what are you doing there?"

I said, "In a nutshell, I help them to have even more fun."

"Really? How?"

"I work as an Agile coach. Agile coaching is all about helping teams to achieve outcome and also have fun at work. I've got to go now. Let us talk about it tomorrow."

That night, I put deep thought into how to stay away from technical jargon while explaining Agile.

#

We met again and he appeared to be very enthusiastic and curious.

Rakesh said, "Ebin, after our conversation, I spoke to two of my friends in IT industry. They're in disagreement with you! One said, 'It is very hectic, high pressure and a mental torture.' The other said, 'We have strict and unrealistic deadlines, most of the time we don't even know what to do or what problem to solve and all blame comes to us.'

"Is this because you happen to work for a super cool company with great policies?"

I smiled. "Did you question them about the other advantages and facilities I mentioned such as, internet, great pay, YouTube, WhatsApp, coffee and tea, etc.?"

He replied, "Of course yes. I reminded both of them about that. They partially agreed and said, "We have all that but who has time to think about those. We are living inside a pressure cooker."

I said, "Okay; that sets a good context for me to introduce what I do, so that you know why organizations are paying people to improve fun at work! Even though people have a lot of freedom and so many facilities, unfortunately, most are not mindful of that. They live in a rabbit hole and are so immersed in their daily work, that they don't even see how blessed they are. By the way, did you probe your friends to understand more about their challenges? Like what is happening to them at work and what is leading them to such a situation?"

He seemed to be waiting for that question, "Yes, I did. This is what I understood:

A) Unrealistic deadlines and targets: The organization always has high expectations, much more than can be accomplished.

B) Communication issues: The customer is not to be seen at all during the development of the product. All of a sudden they appear just to say, 'This is not what we want.' They never say what they want. Even if someone manages to talk to the customer and understand what they are expecting, they keep changing their mind. It is like shooting a moving target.

C) Corporate politics: At the end of the year, we are compared with our teammates to rate our performance. So we not only focus on highlighting our work but also suppress other's work. Since we have to compete with each other within the team, there is not much trust and relationship amongst us.

"Overall I felt that their morale is down and they are demotivated and tired. I also asked about Agile coaching since you mentioned that yesterday. They laughed and said 'we also have some 'jokers' in our company called Agile Coaches. They pour oil to the fire. Always come and increase our burden in the name of Agile by adding new practices and processes.' "

"Wow," I said. "You've done a great deal of research! Most of what you said is very valid. You are talking like an IT professional! I appreciate your communication and articulation skills. You really qualify to become a Product Owner, the person who bridges communication between customer and the team.

"Now that the context is clear, before telling you about the Fun part, let me tell you why Agile is needed. A little background will help you to understand better."

He was in complete agreement. "Yes, Yes. You read my mind."

"Rakesh, let us consider an analogy to understand this better. I think your house construction could be a good one. What do you think?"

Rakesh replied, "Great. I learned so much from the construction experience and I think I'm about to learn even more."

I smiled and asked, "How did you arrive at the final plan of the house?"

Rakesh said, "It took us couple of months. I identified a good architect through a reference. We (me and my wife) had several discussions with him to come to the final plan. Even though we did multiple rounds of changes, the plans kept changing till the end of construction."

I asked him, "Why did those changes happen?"

Rakesh said, "Simple. When we went to meet the architect, our idea was to have a four bedroom house. When the architect started capturing that in the drawings and plans, we started getting more ideas and we started dealing with the granular items like room size, placement of windows, arca for wardrobe, etc. This happened during the construction also because when we saw things shaping up, we made further changes. Later I felt that we shouldn't have spent so much time in detailed planning, rather start the work with a high level plan and take decisions as we see it built and leave the detailing to the architect."

"Perfect. Now let me bring the Agile context to this situation."

Communication

I continued, "What do you think about the importance of communication?"

Rakesh's eyes widened. "Very critical. This is something which can impact the construction from the beginning until the end. The architect should understand what we have in mind and draw the plan, so the way we communicate our need really matters. In the beginning the time spent was more of communication than anything else. I remember a couple of instances where we had to do re–work because the workers understood our need differently."

I liked his observation. I said, "Wonderful. You understand the need for effective communication very well. Now imagine the case of software development. People build on ideas and how customer communicates the idea really matters. If the communication of the idea is not proper or effective, it affects the solution. So, in Agile development methodology, we pay attention to improve the communication layer. We encourage the team to directly talk to the customer or customer representative (Product Owner) as frequently as possible. If there is a possibility, we ask the customer to be with the team so that they can build good relationship and communicate seamlessly."

Rakesh said, "Ok. So *bring the customer close to the team for effective communication*."

I added, "As you mentioned earlier in your

construction example, many times the customer doesn't know what they need. So the best way to bridge the gap is by collaborating with them as much as possible.

"Communication with customer is just one dimension. Another is the software engineers in the team. Communication within teams and between other teams also matters heavily. So we want a mechanism where all involved can communicate seamlessly and frequently."

Rakesh said, "Check. *Enable seamless and frequent communication among and within teams*. So this must be why you guys have social media at work."

Collaboration

I nodded and said, "Let's talk about collaboration now. Collaboration also has multiple dimensions. Unless the architect collaborates with you while accommodating your suggestion and comments, you won't feel comfortable to work with him. If he is not willing to accommodate your changes, you may try to find another architect who is willing to respond to your needs positively."

"Yes. Agreed. Best to have *frequent collaboration with customer*," Rakesh replied in agreement.

I continued, "Another dimension to collaboration is team members. Collaborating with the customer is not good enough. There should be a mechanism to amplify the team collaboration. When they collaborate, the teams learn from each other and grow in maturity. We also have to pay attention to the fact that great trust and respect among individuals will enable collaboration. It is the responsibility of the leadership to provide an environment of trust and respect."

Rakesh said, "So that's what Agile does? It's a system which *encourages collaboration with and within teams*?"

"Yes. Buts it's a philosophy rather than a system. It's

up to you to learn to apply it."

Visibility

"Another important aspect is visibility. How often did you visit your construction site?"

Rakesh answered, "At least five days in a week. Somedays more than once."

"And why did you do that?"

He replied, "I wanted to see the progress. I wanted to ensure that they are doing things as per the specification. During my visits I actually caught couple of deviations, which I could correct immediately."

"Spot on," I continued, "You understand the importance of visibility. It is always better to make the progress visible to the stakeholders, so that you will have right feedback and you can avoid last minute surprises. You can also catch the deviation early, which avoids rework. At regular intervals Agile teams demonstrate to the stakeholders what they have accomplished."

Rakesh jotted down a note. "So we need mechanism to *make progress visible as early as possible*."

Faster Feedback

I felt that Rakesh was getting the concept very fast. I added, "Making the progress visible is just the starting point. What is more important is collecting feedback from the customer/stakeholders. When you see the workers trying to put the window on the wrong side of the wall, you should have a mechanism to give feedback and correct it."

Rakesh nodded and said, "So I just tell them rather than file papers. So Agile people *constantly seek feedback*."

Flexibility / Adaptability

I introduced another dimension. "While the construction was in progress, what did you prefer? A flexible and adaptable system which is ready to receive your comment and act on it, or a rigid system that only executes the original plan?"

Rakesh said, "Of course a flexible system. It is very difficult for us to visualize everything right at the beginning. I think that the plan given by the architect was useful to get started and also to know the boundaries and other specs, but when it comes to the small modifications we wanted during construction, they should be flexible."

I continued, "Good. Another interesting example is driving during traffic hours. If you have a flexible mindset you will choose the road according to traffic conditions. If you look at google maps, it will give you multiple options to choose from, depending on different conditions. So people by nature prefer flexibility and adaptability."

Rakesh said, "Yes, *be flexible and respond to the feedback*. If the environment changes, this is an obvious need."

Risk

I asked, "Rakesh, what do you think about risk now?"

"If the system is visible and constantly taking feedback and acting on it, I think the risk of going wrong is very less."

I liked his answer. I added, "Exactly. Make the system visible at each level of its progress and constantly take feedback, so that the risk reduces. However, in software industry there are other risks such as knowledge risk, social risk, technical risk. When the team continuously makes the system visible and collects feedback from the customer all these risks are minimized. High collaborative environment also will give people an opportunity to deliberately look at the risks and mitigate them.

"Another important concept in software industry is time to market. How early you send the product to market is a key success factor because of the tight competition and dynamic market. So people look at what the Minimum Marketable Features—MMFs—are, and build it faster and release the product with those MMFs. They also consider adding more features later based on user inputs and feedback. It is more like how you find out what minimum livable facilities are required in the house."

Rakesh said, "I got it. In fact, I used to think about that. If we didn't bother about furnishing our house to a perceived perfect state, we could have moved in at least four months earlier. Now I know why my mobile phone keeps reminding me about the latest OS update. They have added new features beyond the MMF. I think I am learning some software jargon now.

"So I'm adding to my notes: A way of working that *enables us to reduce the time to market.*"

Predictability
Exactly, I continued, "Predictability is another factor which is very critical. Predictability enables us to make forecast. When the system is predictable, we could also project our time to market.

"In the case of house construction, one example could be that you can forecast how much money you need for the construction in different phases and also how early or late that phase is going to be."

Rakesh said, "Very true. In fact, I had to change my forecast twice because of the unpredictable behavior of my carpenters. We had planned to do our house warming much earlier.

"So we want to *enable predictability and forecasting.*"

Value

Now it was time to talk about value. I said, "Another area is value creation. Even though value is one of the key dimensions, I didn't mention that earlier because we need to talk about other things to set the stage for this. Most of the mentioned criteria such as collaboration, visibility, faster feedback, flexibility, etc. will enable the teams to create the most valuable features first. The customer chooses the order of what features to deliver first by considering what items are most valuable."

Rakesh commented, "I understand that. Now I can connect to the recent changes made by the satellite TV operators. I can choose the channel I wish to watch and pay only for that. I really love the idea. As a customer I feel that I have got more power now. Aha! They are also Agile!"

"Exactly." I liked his analogy. "In software industry there is another advantage. If there is a feature which is a 'shipment stopper,' we can choose to build that first so that we can take a better decision on the future plans. The flexibility to add most valuable feature first will help the organization to reduce their time to market as well."

Rakesh said, "Ok. Our system should allow the *customer to participate in prioritization.*"

Quality

"You got it right." I really liked his statement. "Another aspect to consider is quality."

Rakesh intervened, "Let me guess. When the progress is visible to the customer and when we collaborate with them on a daily basis we improve the quality. Since the workers knew that I may visit the site anytime during the construction, they don't compromise on quality. Couple of times there were discussions about using some low quality material which was faster and easier to procure. I clarified to them that I care for my house."

"Well said," I added. "That is a very valid point. When the stakeholder shows care, it will pass on to the people involved as well. Agile promotes *self–organization and cross–functionality*, which enables a high degree of ownership for the team."

Learning

I asked Rakesh, "Now can you tell me where you see learning here?"

Rakesh held out both hands and waved them in circles. "Everywhere! The collaboration with customer will give learning about customer need. Visibility and Feedback gives learning on how they are progressing. I see an opportunity for learning everywhere."

"Very good," I continued "In fact, because learning is so critical, the system should be *designed for learning*.

"I think we pretty much covered the 'Why Agile.' What do you think now?"

Rakesh said, "Ebin, things are very clear. Now I am wondering what is there which is so special about software industry. I feel that all what we have discussed is normal human need and commonsense."

I replied, "That is a very valid observation. I didn't talk about the manifesto so far. Now I am curious to know how you will react when I explain to you the 'Agile Manifesto[5].' "

"The first value in the manifesto is, 'Individual and Interaction over processes and tools.' This essentially means that people and their interaction are more important than processes and tools. When we talk about

---

5 AgileManifesto.org

people and interaction, we are stressing on values such as, respect, trust, transparency, relationship, and focus on face to face communication. Remember that processes and tools are also important but priority is for the individuals and interactions. If we don't have good interactions and relationship among team members we can't achieve good result in the long run.

"The second value in manifesto is, 'Working software over comprehensive documentation.' This essentially means that, teams should focus on delivering value to the customer by incrementally developing the product and produce just enough documentation. Traditional development used to produce tons of documentation even before the start of creation/ manufacture of the product. It is a reminder to focus on customer need and intrinsic quality and make sure that documents produced by the teams are valuable. What would you prefer? A working program with some features or 'a book' describing how the whole system works! Remember it is not about 'No Documentation,' it is about necessary documentation.

"The third value in manifesto is, 'Customer Collaboration over Contract Negotiation.' Customers are not some alien beings. The best solution emerges when we work together with the customer. When we uphold values like, Trust, Transparency, Open Communication, etc. with the customer, better collaboration emerges. This should lead to a constructive partnership with the customer. When you collaborate with customer, you get frequent feedback from the customer, which leads to great products and high customer satisfaction. We should invest in building good, transparent relations with the customer and avoid caging the customer with contract documents. Of course contracts and legal documents are needed but we should give priority to collaboration so that the best solution emerges. Remember, our customer's success is our success.

"The fourth value is 'Responding to change over following a plan.' This tells us to be open to changes when the environment or business problems change. We should evolve the product. The assumptions made at the time of initial planning will/may change as we progress. We should be always open to consider how we can adapt and be flexible to the situation, so that, we can solve the customer problems effectively. Remember 'Planning is useful, plans are useless!' Focus should be always on adding value to the customer, not on a plan which was created with limited understanding and a lot of assumptions which has changed during the course of time.

"So, how do you like the Agile Manifesto?"

Rakesh answered, "Well, as I mentioned earlier, it is more of human values and common sense than anything else."

Rakesh looked at his watch and realized that he is getting late. He asked me, "We started this discussion because you said 'Agile software development is fun!' So how do you drive home that point?"

"Ah." I took a deep breath and answered, "Let me tell you what I mean by that. We have had a great discussion about why Agile, what is Agile, the values and principles of Agile and the Agile Manifesto. When we discussed those, multiple times you mentioned that it is basic fundamental human values and principle and 'nothing software about it.' We have also seen real world examples of how Agile we are in all walks of our life, be it house construction, or the traffic, or our personal relationships. Can you recall all those fundamental values we discussed?"

"Of course I shall!" Rakesh started, "Trust, respect, collaboration, learning, transparency, open communication, good relationships, courage, commitment, openness, focus, and flexibility."

"Wow, I am impressed." I was amazed by his answer. "Wonderful. Now can you tell me where you see all these in action in your life?"

Rakesh didn't have to think much before answering. "In my family. I think in our family we value all these. With our close friends as well."

"Exactly! If I may ask you to recall the best moment in your life what would that be?"

"It is the time I spend with my family and friends," Rakesh answered immediately.

I was happy with the answer. "Super. Have you ever wondered why is it so? In my perspective we, any human being, love to be in a place where we are respected, valued, and trusted. When there is trust and respect, relationship and bonding emerges. We feel courageous and committed. We also see that a common belief system emerges. You get a sense of belonging. You will have real fun and joy. A good work–life balance."

"I see Agile principles and practices as an opportunity to get these basics right for our life at work as well."

I nodded. "What happens if all your teammates become your best friends and you feel valued and trusted and respected?"

"Wow, that will be amazing. I would love to go to office every day!" Rakesh said immediately.

I paused for a while then asked, "And?"

Rakesh was very quick to catch it. He said, "We will have fun and Joy."

"Awesome. You said it!" I continued, "I hope Agile has given you more ideas to have fun and joy at work."

Rakesh thought deeply then replied, "Yes it has. Ebin, I really feel like being an Agile Coach!"

WHY LET YOUR FRAMEWORK LIMIT YOU?

by Deepak Dhananjaya & Gunjan Zutshi

What is now happening in the world of Agile is a typical case of the tail wagging the dog. The majority of Agile transformations are being driven by frameworks (Scrum, Kanban, . . .) rather than needs of the organization. The framework is decided first and then goals of the transformation are looked at. In doing so, what should have been centre stage—the need of the system engaging in transformation—becomes a side line and the framework the 'Hero.'

Another missing link is lack of attention to the whole. Change is brought at an individual or team level without looking holistically at the entire system. Organizations are open systems (a system that interacts dynamically with its environment) and what happens in one subsystem has an impact on other sub systems. Thinking of Agile transformations as merely process implementation is a myopic view. Just implementing frameworks and rituals is like saying that loosing weight is being healthy. Being healthy is more holistic than loosing weight, and so is being Agile. Transformations are complete only when they become a way of life—'being Agile' rather than 'doing Agile.'

This dissatisfaction with how Agile implementations are being looked at, and a desire to find a holistic, systemic approach to transformation, brought us (Gunjan and Deepak) together. Two diverse individuals—a hard core techie and Agile evangelist, and an organisation development practitioner—to try to find some answers.

Over numerous cups of tea and discussions, we talked over our years of experience implementing change at large enterprises and concluded that transformations are not just about implementing a set of steps from a framework or making changes in the process of doing work. Change is more effective when the whole system is involved in the process. There is a shared discovery of needs, aspirations, and goals which become the primary drivers for transformation and help decide what frameworks are best for the context.

Agile transformations need to address all aspects of change be effective and sustainable. The aim is to get the organization to develop capabilities to see the whole system and not just 'my part.' Managing the social aspect of change is as important as managing the technical aspect of change.

System Driven Transformation (SDT)—A systemic and framework agnostic approach to Agile transformations

Blending our understanding of the Agile Manifesto, Agile frameworks, and Organization Development, we built a system driven, humanistic approach to Agile transformations.

The result was "System Driven Transformation (SDT)." Just like Test Driven Development (TDD) is a way of understanding the goals of the product code before you write it, System Driven Transformation is a similar approach for understanding an Agile transformation.

A fundamental tenet is to be framework agnostic. It requires detachment from prematurely selecting a solution. This does not mean there isn't structure or that there is chaos. It only means that the system defines its own framework/working method that is most effective for its circumstance. This allows us to keep the needs of the system centre stage rather than impose frameworks without first understanding the goals of the system.

For this to happen, some boundary conditions are required which are provided by the values mentioned in the Agile Manifesto (www.AgileManifesto.org). These values are critical to 'being Agile' and provide guidelines within which transformation can take place.

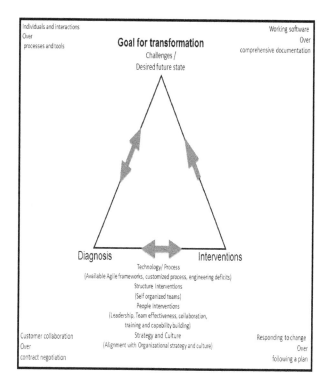

Instead of starting with the question of which framework to use, we first ask, what is the goal for transformation? These goals become what the system desires as outcome of Agile transformation. It is formulated by considering: the current state of the system, and challenges the system is facing or characteristics that the system wants. This everything that is done as part of transformation process must support those goals.

A critical part of clarifying the goal and deciding interventions is diagnosis. It is to understand not just what can be seen—the issues / problems / challenges—which are merely the symptoms, but also to figure out the underlying reasons for these challenges. It involves diagnosis of technology / process (current software development process, engineering deficits), structure (organization / team), people (leadership, collaboration, capability), and culture or strategy (context for change).

The next step in our approach is to work along with stakeholders to determine the interventions. There can be many ways to achieve the goal. Solutions are guided by the values of Agile Manifesto and not constrained by any single Agile framework. The solution may involve using any existing Agile framework, a combination of frameworks, or a unique framework developed by keeping in view the needs of the system. Interventions focus on structure and people aspects of transformation so that the change effort is holistic and sustainable.

In keeping with the spirit of Agile, this is not a linear approach. Rather, based on principles of Action Research (Lewin, 1944), it requires constant validation and feedback to check what is working and what needs to change. Every step feeds backward and forward so that actions are real time keeping pace with changing context and needs.

In our work so far with using SDT as a working methodology, we find that many times, the goal for transformation itself is not clearly articulated. Helping organizations clarify this opens up many ways in which to work in implementing the transformation.

Another area SDT adds immense value is to diagnose not just at the process or technology level, but to look at all aspects that may impact transformation. Most often, these conversations pave the way for creating a shared understanding of what needs to be done and plan for changes needed at each socio–technical levels. By integrating concepts from other fields like Transactional Analysis, Group Relations, Open Systems Theory, and Appreciative Inquiry, we get a deeper understanding of organisations as systems and the resulting dynamics at play. This understanding in turn ensures that the processes of change are not obstructed unintentionally and change is sustainable.

Systems Driven Transformation has yielded positive results for us and our clients. We are sure that there are others who think like us (or may be not and that too is OK!) and we would love to hear from you. If you would like to share your feedback or experiences, do write to us at deepak@agilesattva.com and gunjan@agilesattva.com, and visit us at www.AgileSattva.com.

ABOUT THE AUTHOR

Lancer Kind lives in Seattle, Xiamen China, and spaces in between. He started his IT career in 1995 then after four years of Waterfall his team was introduced to eXtreme Programming by Kent Beck and achieved the ability to make a "ship or no–ship" decision within four hours through the use of automated unit and system tests. In 2006 he began Agile coaching and training technical practices. For the last ten years he has delivered consulting services in China, India, as well as the USA, and has spoken at Agile conferences at all of the aforementioned. He's a publishing author of science fiction and of a project management comic series called Scrum Noir which for a week was the best selling book on project management.

Lancer produces the Agile Thoughts podcast and blogs about Agile at AgileNoir.biz and science fiction at LancerKind.com. You can send him a tweet about whatever is on your mind at: @LancerKind

SCRUM NOIR

Each issue loaded with Agile knowledge in a way that's fun to read. Available in ebook and print at book sellers online and off.

SCIENCE FICTION

Award winning science fiction by Lancer Kind.

AGILE THOUGHTS PODCAST

Level up your delivery with some Agile thoughts! Learn the skills necessary to deliver IS solutions like those described in Agile Noir. These are skills any team or organization can learn if they have the motivation.

Made in the USA
Middletown, DE
12 May 2021